T0016355

THE **MINI** ROUGH GUIDE TO
KEFALONIÁ

YOUR TAILOR-MADE TRIP
STARTS HERE

Tailor-made trips and unique adventures crafted by local experts

Rough Guides has been inspiring travellers for more than 35 years. Leave it to our local experts to create your perfect itinerary and book it at local rates.

Don't follow the crowd – find your own path.

HOW ROUGHGUIDES.COM/TRIPS WORKS

STEP 1 Pick your dream destination, tell us what you want and submit an enquiry.

STEP 2 Fill in a short form to tell your local expert about your dream trip and preferences.

STEP 3 Our local expert will craft your tailor-made itinerary. You'll be able to tweak and refine it until you're completely satisfied.

STEP 4 Book online with ease, pack your bags and enjoy the trip! Our local expert will be on hand 24/7 while you're on the road.

PLAN AND BOOK YOUR TRIP AT
ROUGHGUIDES.COM/TRIPS

HOW TO DOWNLOAD YOUR FREE EBOOK

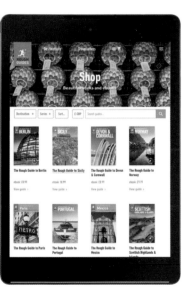

1. Visit **www.roughguides.com/free-ebook** or scan the **QR code** below

2. Enter the code **kefalonia356**

3. Follow the simple step-by-step instructions

For troubleshooting contact: mail@roughguides.com

10 THINGS NOT TO MISS

A PERFECT TOUR

Day 1

Argostóli and Lixoúri. Start with a coffee on Argostóli's central Platía Valliánou. Then stroll down Lithóstroto, detouring to take in the Korgialénios History and Folklore Museum before lunch at Tzivras. Later take your rental car across to Lixoúri, hitting Xi or Kounópetra beach. Back in Argostóli, have supper at waterfront Kyani Akti before bed.

Day 2

Argostóli and Lássi. Another day in and around Argostóli: visiting the Gentilini winery beyond Lássi, the Focas-Kosmetátou Foundation exhibition in town and then across the gulf to Lixoúri and beyond to Petaní beach for lunch at Xouras taverna and a well-deserved dip in the sea, before returning to base. Have dinner at Casa Grec in Argostóli.

Day 3

South coast. Head across the Livathó plain, pausing at Kástro Ágios Geórgios before a dip at Ávythos or Lourdháta beach. Next stop is the Orealios Gaea Wine Co-op, followed by a drive up Mount Énos to view the native firs. Enjoy lunch at Káto Katélios, and stay the night at Skála resort.

Day 4

Skála. Take in the Roman villa floor mosaics at Skála before continuing northwest to visit the Melissáni and Dhrogaráti caves, and then lunching in Sámi or Agía Evfimía. Cross the island via Dhivaráta to Ássos where you overnight.

Day 5

Ássos. Enjoy the castle and a swim before departing north towards Fiskárdho. En route, detour to Agía Ierousalím for

...unch at Odysseas and perhaps another dip before arriving at Fiskárdho, where you have dinner and stay overnight.

Day 6

Boat trip. Rent a small boat to reach a nearby beach – perhaps Fokí or Dhafnoúdhi – where you spend the middle of the day prior to another overnight and dinner in Fiskárdho.

Day 7

Ágia Evfimía and Itháki. Leave Fiskárdho, heading south along the easterly road through Neohóri, arriving at Ágia Evfimía in time for a swim and lunch at Amalia taverna before boarding the ferry from Sámi to Pisaetós on Itháki. Missed the last daily ferry (likely)? No problem, overnight in Sámi, having dinner at *Akrogiali* or Karnagio tavernas.

Day 8

Vathý. Safely arrived on Itháki, settle into your hotel before lunch at *Trehantiri* and, if feeling energetic, take a walk to the southerly Odysseus sites, or more lazily a dip at one of the pebble beaches such as Sarakíniko Dinner at *To Kohili*.

Day 9

Stávros and around. Explore the north of Itháki by car. Stávros has a worthwhile museum and a good lunch tavern (*O Tseligas*); have a swim at beautiful Afáles beach before dinner in Fríkes (*Odysseus taverna*) or Kióni (*Avra taverna*) prior to another overnight in Vathý.

Day 10

Back to Argostóli. Return to Kefaloniá by ferry in time for your flight home, dropping your rental car at the airport.

CONTENTS

HIGHLIGHTS

OVERVIEW

Located in the sun-drenched Ionnian Islands, Kefaloniá has a somewhat forbidding and mountainous landscape but with it comes beautiful inlets sheltered by steep rocky enclaves, long sandy beaches and mesmerising coastal drives. As with most Greek islands, the people are welcoming and hospitable – although rival island neighbours have been known to say that Kefaloniáns are more reserved and eccentric. A famous local legend helps to somewhat explain this point of view. It tells of Lixoúri satirist Andreas Laskaratos whose impiety prompted the local bishop to excommunicate him, which among other things meant that he would lie incorruptible in his grave and be liable to become a vampire. Laskaratos' response was to beg the bishop to also excommunicate his favourite pair of boots, so that they too would last forever.

Following the devastating earthquake of the 1950s, there was a large wave of emigration to North America and Africa, and the subsequent departure of islanders in search of work on the mainland, has borne its scars over the years. But interestingly, those who

MYTHICAL ORIGINS

According to Greek mythology, Taphios, the son of Poseidon and the sea-nymph Hippothoë, established the city of Taphos on the Peloponnese. Under his son Pterelaos this expanded to include the nearby Ionian islands, and so the inhabitants of Kefaloniá became known as Taphioi. The present-day name is said to come from Kephalos (Cephalus) – a son of the king of Ileia – and the names of the four ancient cities (see page 15) from his four sons: Kranios, Palevs, Pronessos and Samos.

leave are steadily replaced by returning emigres who've made their fortune and with people from other islands in search of a better life; ensuring a pleasant continuity and natural balance on the island, testament to its enduring appeal.

GEOLOGY AND ENVIRONMENT

One evident attribute of the island is its unique and important natural environ-

Sacred snakes

The most famous Kefaliniá snakes are the small, harmless specimens which emerge most years in Markópoulo village between 7 and 15 August, the festival of the Dormition of the Mother of God. They have a small cross-shaped mark on their head and, if they fail to appear on time, it is considered a bad omen for the year concerned.

ment. The sea around Kefaloniá is beautifully clean, crystal clear and home to a small population of rare Mediterranean monk seals and one of the most endangered species to be found in Greek waters: the loggerhead turtle.

Kefaloniá is formed predominantly of hard Cretaceous limestone riddled with many caves, and is separated from the other Ionian islands to the north by the Kefaloniá fault zone. The heavily folded rock points to a turbulent geological history, and Kefaloniá's position along the Hellenic Subduction Zone gives rise to numerous earthquakes.

Kefaloniá has an area of 780 sq km (302 sq miles), making it the largest of the seven Ionian Islands, which extend from Corfu in the north to Zákynthos in the southeast. Along with its small, co-governed neighbour Itháki (96 sq km/37 sq miles), the population is just under 38,000.

As well as being home to several species of mammal (including martens, *Martes foina*, and – on Mount Énos – endangered feral ponies, of which barely a dozen remain), Kefaloniá has a number of interesting reptiles. One of the most spectacular is the large but non-venomous Aesculapian rat snake (*Zamenis longissimus*), which can grow up to 2 metres (6.5ft) in length; of a similar size is the Montpellier snake (*Malpolon monspessulanus*), another harmless rodent- and lizard-catcher.

Among birds of prey, you may spot Eleonora's falcons swooping about the cliffs of the north and west coasts, and little owls (*Athena noctua*), often visible and audible by day, perched on utility wires and ruined buildings. At night, listen out for the tiny Scops owl (*Otus scops*), more often heard than seen (its distinctive, repetitive peeping like a submarine's sonar), and barn owls (*Tito alba*). Smaller birds include the woodchat shrike, (*Lanius senator*), the house martin (*Delichon urbicum*) and the beautiful golden oriole

Melissáni cave lake

(*Oriolus oriolus*). Three kinds of warbler can be found in scrubland or agricultural areas.

TOURISM

The history of tourism on Kefaloniá is less invasive than on other Ionian islands, such as Corfu or Zákynthos. The relatively low-key tourist developments that do exist are mainly concentrated in Lássi just outside of Argostóli, and at Lourdháta, Skála and Káto Kateliós in

The loggerhead turtle

the southeast. The main boost to Kefaloniá's tourism industry came during the mid-1990s with the phenomenal success of the book by Louis de Bernières (and subsequent film) *Captain Corelli's Mandolin* (see page 47). The descriptions of idyllic, pre-World-War-II island life inspired a large number of visitors to come and see for themselves, though because of its unflattering portrayal of the local communist resistance, the book is mostly disliked on Kefaloniá. Generally fairly affluent, these visitors (mainly from Italy and the UK) have encouraged high-end, and therefore more expensive, development. These tend to be visually kinder to the landscape, though this has resulted in some places, Fiskárdho in particular, becoming overly twee.

ISLAND LIFE

Outside the peak months of July and August life carries on much as it does elsewhere in Greece. Many people still grow olives and grapes, the harvest for both crops taking place between late August and January. Local fishermen (as well as intruding Italian fleets) have severely depleted the Ionian/Adriatic seas of swordfish in particular through the use of large, mechanised trawlers.

A number of the local tavernas, at least in the capital and the main ports Sámi and Póros, stay open throughout the winter, and this is the time when islanders tend to go out and enjoy themselves after the hard work of the tourist season. This division of the year does lead to high seasonal unemployment, and some people move to the mainland – or overseas – during the winter. Aside from fishing and agriculture there is little else in terms of enterprise on Kefaloniá – aside from the odd quarry or small-scale food processing – but talk of trying to expand the tourist season, such as offering spring treks to see the local flora, has failed to materialise on a significant level.

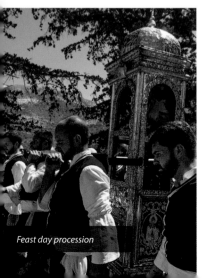

Feast day procession

One traditional aspect of life that still continues is the singing of *kandádes*. These are songs performed by a group of male singers with a guitar and mandolin accompaniment. The music itself is a combination of local traditional songs, Italian popular songs and 19th-century operatic arias (a legacy of Venetian rule). It is not at all unusual to hear Neapolitan favourites such as *O sole mio* in amongst Greek offerings.

HISTORY AND CULTURE

Evidence of early human settlement on the southern Ionian Islands is scarce. There has been little excavation of specifically Palaeolithic and Neolithic sites, though a number of artefacts, such as flint hand tools, have been found, some of which are on display in Argostóli's archaeological museum. The earliest human presence is thought to date from the mid-Palaeolithic era (c.50,000 years ago), when, due to ice-age reduction in sea levels, the Ionians were joined to present-day Greece and Italy. It is thought that hunter-gatherer groups arrived in the region, probably searching for food, from the Píndos (northern Greece) and the Peloponnese. Some of these groups then settled on what is now the island of Kefaloniá.

THE BRONZE AGE

Archaeologists know that there was a thriving Mycenean society on Kefaloniá. It is assumed, backed up by artefacts found during excavations, that the four city-states of ancient Kefaloniá have their origins in the Late-Helladic period of c.1500–1050 BC. One of the major centres on Kefaloniá appears to have been near Tzanáta in the southeast, about 8km (5 miles) from the site of Pronesos, of interest due to its possible links to Odysseus. Other important sites on Kefaloniá include the chamber tombs at Mazarakáta,

Ancient Divisions

Ancient Kefaloniá was a tetrapolis, comprised of four independent city-states. These were: Pali on the present-day Palikí Peninsula, Krani near Dhrápano, Sámi near the eponymous modern port, and Pronesos on the southeast coast.

The Mycenean tholos tomb near Tzanáta

(first excavated by C.P. de Bosset in 1813), Metaxáta and Lakíthra, the last of which yielded the richest finds of any of the island's Bronze-Age tombs.

THE ARCHAIC, CLASSICAL AND HELLENISTIC PERIODS

The origins of the city-states of Kefaloniá are the subjects of Greek mythology (see page 10), but they were also mentioned by the ancient Greek historians Herodotus and Thucydides.

On Kefaloniá, the city-states were generally politically independent of each other and formed their own alliances; Pali alone fought in the Persian Wars, at the battle of Plataea (479 BC). However, up until the Peloponnesian War they were all to a greater or lesser extent – but particularly Pali – allied to Corinth. Krani also had links to the Athenians and, upon the outbreak of the Peloponnesian War, the whole island was brought under the sphere of Athens.

At some point during the Archaic and Classical periods (from c.750 BC) the Kefalonian city-states became democratic. It is known that citizens of the Kefalonian *demos* who were eligible to vote (which excluded women and slaves) took part in political decision-making, and that the *boule* (municipal council) was the 'dominant institution' in the city of Pali. Scholars of ancient Greece have also observed that none of the coins from the city-states showed an image of a ruler (except for that of the mythical founder Kephalos; see page 10).

During the Peloponnesian War (431–404 BC) the Kefalonian cities wavered in their allegiance between Sparta and Athens, and in 226 BC became members of the Aetolic marine confederation. Subsequently, the imperial Macedonian tenure on Kefaloniá was fleeting. The end of Hellenistic influence came when the Roman General Marcus Fulvius Nobilior conquered Kefaloniá in 189 BC.

THE BYZANTINES AND FRANKS

From the point of the Roman acquisition to the advent of Byzantine rule in 337 AD little of note is recorded in Kefalonian history. However, the archaeological record shows a certain degree of wealth and artistic activity, as at the villa at Skála (see page 40).

ODYSSEUS

The Homeric epic *The Odyssey* follows the adventures of its hero Odysseus from Troy, on the coast of Anatolia, back home to mythical Ithaca. For a long time it was assumed that Ithaca was present-day Itháki, where numerous local features were named after events in the epic. However, there is no archaeological evidence to back these claims and the latest thinking points to southern Kefaloniá as the most likely spot for Odysseus' kingdom.

Under the Byzantines, Kefaloniá became active in defending the empire against attack from Arab pirates, and, in 850, it became the head of the *theme*, or administrative district, which also included Zákynthos, Lefkádha and Corfu.

As Byzantine power waned, attacks on all of the Ionian islands became more common. In 1085 Robert Guiscard, a Norman leader, attacked Fiskárdo and by 1185 Kefaloniá was under the rule of the Franks (a diverse group of largely Norman and Italian nobility). They were at first headed by the Venetian Orsini family, to whom the island passed after the Fourth Crusade in 1204. In 1357 it was granted, by the King of Naples, to the Tocco family, whose most remarkable member was Francesca Acciaioli, widow of Carlo I, who reigned after his death in 1429, albeit for just a single year, setting up an all-female court in Kástro Agios Geóryios. (see page 36).

The Venetian fort at Ássos

OTTOMANS AND VENETIANS

With the growing power of the Ottoman Turks to the east, it was inevitable that the Ionian Islands would receive their attention and, in 1479, the warlord Gedik Ahmad Pasha overran Kefaloniá, taking many prisoners back to Istanbul. Although the Venetians, then the other major force in the eastern Mediterranean, briefly regained Kefaloniá in 1481, it was ceded back to Sultan Beyazit II by treaty in 1485.

The Venetians were not deterred from ideas of Mediterranean domination, however. In 1500 they attacked Kefaloniá with the help of a Spanish army and, after a two-month siege, took control of Kástro Ágios Yeóryios on Christmas Day. Thus, apart from a brief period, Kefaloniá and the other Ionian islands (except for Lefkádha) are among the few areas of Greece not to have come under prolonged Ottoman rule or been noticeably influenced by it.

The Ionian Islands remained under the Venetians until 1797. This was a period of relative calm, although the Venetians ensured that both Zákynthos and Kefaloniá were heavily defended; the impressive castles at Ássos and Ágios Yeóryios (the long-time Venetian capital) on Kefaloniá are a legacy of Venetian rule. Not only were the Ionian Islands prized as staging posts for the Venetian navy, they were also useful for their agricultural production, and most of the olive trees now seen here were planted during this time.

One of the most visible legacies of the Venetian occupation is the large number of splendid churches, many with ornate, gilded baroque interiors. Much of the churches' interior decoration, and many of their icons, is the work of Cretan sculptors and painters, who fled to Zákynthos and Kefaloniá after the last Venetian stronghold on Crete fell to the Ottomans in 1669. Once on the islands, they came under the influence of the Italian Renaissance and the resulting artistic synthesis is known as painting of the Ionian School.

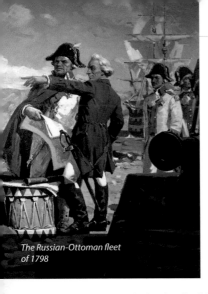
The Russian-Ottoman fleet of 1798

Local rulers came from aristocratic Venetian families, who acquired large estates after settling on the Ionian Islands. Their names were inscribed in the so-called *Libro d'Oro* (Golden Book) on each island, as members of the highest of three social classes; the others being a nascent bourgeoisie, with limited political rights, and the *popolari* or oppressed peasantry, with none. The Greek Orthodox Church assumed an inferior position to the Catholic Church, although local women who married Venetian men were not forced to convert to Catholicism.

The language of the upper classes and of literature was Italian, or dialects thereof. Despite marginally improved living conditions, the Ionian islanders were not immune from rumblings of nationalist discontent that grew steadily louder through the 18th century.

THE SEPTINSULAR REPUBLIC AND THE BRITISH

Discontent became more evident when, in 1797, the islands were occupied by the revolutionary French, who saw their potential as a strategic naval base. By decree, Napoleon abolished all Venetian feudal privileges – the *Libro d'Oro* was burnt in public squares on the main islands – and the revolutionary fervour with which the islanders greeted the invaders initially went into radical proposals such as the abolition of organised religion. However, rival powers, specifically the Orthodox Russians, were unhappy about

Napoleon's widening sphere of influence and agitation against the French began to ferment. In 1798 a joint Russian-Ottoman fleet sailed for the islands and, with local support, they fell easily to the invaders, who restored the privileges of the old nobility. The subsequent Treaty of Constantinople, signed in 1800, ushered in the creation of an autonomous republic under Turkish suzerainty.

This, the Eptánisos Politía (Septinsular Republic), became the first, nominally, independent modern Greek state. The fledgling state came to an end in 1807, when the islands reverted to the French under the Treaty of Tilsit, and in turn Kefaloniá was occupied by the British in 1809; by 1814 they had taken possession of all the Ionian islands. The British occupation, which lasted until 1864, was not an entirely happy time for the islanders. The first Lord High Commissioner, Thomas Maitland, was dubbed 'the Abortion'

Monument to the British administration in Argostóli

by the islanders, on account of his rudeness, aversion to personal hygiene and attempts to interfer with Ionian assistance to the Greek insurrectionists on the mainland during the 1820s. Although the British did carry out a number of still-used public works on the larger islands, the local population became increasingly unhappy about foreign occupation and rule, especially after the creation of the neighbouring modern Greek state in 1828–31. Although the largely complicit urban middle class had a comfortable standard of living, the peasant farmers were as downtrodden and poor as they had been under Venetian domination. The local island press agitated ceaselessly against British rule.

INDEPENDENCE

The Ionian islands had long been a place of refuge for independence fighters from the mainland, and in 1864 the islanders' nationalist ambitions were finally realised when the British ceded all of the Ionian islands to Greece, as a condition for Danish Prince William of the Glücksberg dynasty ascending the Greek throne as King George I.

Ioannis Metaxas

The enlightenment ideals that had spurred the islanders to agitate for independence, or at least union, with Greece manifested themselves in radical politics. Kefaloniá in particular was

the birthplace of Marinos Antypas (born 1872), the 'first Greek socialist', who was murdered in Thessaly in 1907. A more disturbing side of this penchant for extremism manifested in the fascist dictator Ioannis Metaxas, another native of Kefaloniá, who ruled Greece from a military coup in 1936 until his death in 1941, three months before the German invasion of Greece.

WORLD WAR II AND THE 1953 EARTHQUAKE

As in most of Europe, World War II proved a catastrophe for the Ionians. Although the Greeks initially repulsed Mussolini's army in 1940–41, driving them deep back into Albania, a more powerful joint German-Bulgarian force overran Greece during 1941. All of the Ionian islands were initially under the Italians but when Italy capitulated to the Allies in September 1943, the Germans replaced them on their former territories, imposing a far more brutal regime. On Kefaloniá, between 22–26 September, the Germans executed

Tourists on Antisamos beach

almost the entire Italian Acqui Division for refusing to continue the war on the Axis side – an episode vividly fictionalised in the film starring Nicholas Cage and Penélope Cruz set on the island, *Captain Corelli's Mandolin* (see page 47)

Kefaloniá had just begun to recover from the joint effects of World War II and the ensuing Greek Civil War when, on 12 August 1953, it was struck by a huge earthquake. The epicentre was on the seabed between Zákynthos and Kefaloniá, so the impact was felt more in the southern, settled parts of Kefaloniá, and the northern part of Zákynthos, which was relatively unpopulated. The devastation on Kefaloniá was almost total – except for the far north – and over 400 people were killed. Now began a new wave of emigration, both internal and overseas, in particular to Australia, Canada, Sudan, the Belgian Congo and South Africa.

THE ARRIVAL OF TOURISM

Compared to neighbouring Zákynthos, Kefaloniá was relatively ignored until the phenomenal success of *Captain Corelli's Mandolin* brought numerous tourists to the island during the 1990s, at the same time as emigré Kefalonians began to return from abroad. The advent of budget airline services from the UK in the early 2000s made it easier for independent tourists to arrive on Kefaloniá and it continues to be an idyllic holiday destination.

IMPORTANT DATES

c.50,000 BC Evidence of Palaeolithic settlement.

c.1500–1050 BC Establishment of the four city-states of Kefaloniá.

189 BC Conquest of the island by the Romans.

AD 337 The islands come under Byzantine rule.

1185–1479 Unopposed Frankish occupation of the Ionian islands.

1479 Ottomans overrun Kefaloniá, taking many locals prisoner.

1500 The Ottomans are expelled by a joint Venetian-Spanish force, ensuring the Ionian islands (except for Lefkádha) are among the few areas of Greece to remain free of Ottoman influence.

1500–1797 Venetian era sees the appearance of distinctive churches, sumptuous townhouses and vast olive plantations.

1797 The islands are occupied by the revolutionary French.

1798 Russians and Ottomans take the islands from the French.

1800 Treaty of Constantinople. The Eptánisos Politía (State of the Seven Islands) becomes the first modern Greek state, under Russo-Ottoman control.

1807 Treaty of Tilsit; Ionian Islands revert to the French.

1809–64 British occupation of the islands.

1864 Ionian Islands are ceded to Greece with the reign of King George I.

1941–4 World War II. Ionian islands are occupied initially by Italians, then Germans; in September 1943, over 5,000 Italian soldiers are executed on Kefaloniá in what becomes known as the Massacre of the Acqui Division.

1953 Huge earthquake hits Kefaloniá, killing over 400 people.

1980s First package tours arrive on Kefaloniá.

2000 *Captain Corelli's Mandolin* is filmed on Kefaloniá.

2015 Alexis Tsipras, of the far-left Syriza Party, becomes PM as head of a coalition, but accedes to the demands of creditors to avoid bankruptcy.

2016 Greece agrees a rescue deal with creditors.

2019 Kyriakos Mitsotakis' centre-right New Democracy party in power.

2020–21 Covid-19 pandemic wreaks havoc on two tourist seasons.

2022 Having demonstrated sustained financial probity, Greece exits its creditors' 'supervision'. Record year for tourist arrivals from overseas.

2023 National elections scheduled.

The Sacred Monastery of
Agios Gerasimos

OUT AND ABOUT

KEFALONIÁ

Dramatic, rugged and mountainous, Kefaloniá is the largest and highest Ionian island, rising to 1,627m (5,338ft) at the summit of Mount Énos. Although, or perhaps because, tourism is a relatively recent phenomenon on the island, sparked off in part by the book and film, *Captain Corelli's Mandolin* (see page 47), Kefaloniá has one of the least spoilt environments and some of the best beaches in the Ionian Islands. The south is dominated by the heights of Mount Énos, bordered on the west by the Livathó Plain. In the west is the quiet Palikí Peninsula, while the stunning north coast is fringed by dramatic cliffs.

ARGOSTÓLI

The island's capital, and also its largest town, **Argostóli** ❶ was completely destroyed in the 1953 earthquake and has been rebuilt largely as modern concrete buildings. Although it serves primarily as a port and administrative centre, the town is not entirely devoid of charm. It has a great position on a bay within a bay surrounded by mountains, as well as a number of interesting museums, and it makes a good base for exploring the rest of the island. Life in Argostóli centres around

Seismic emigration

The 1953 earthquake devastated almost all of Kefaloniá – except the far north – causing a huge exodus of emigrants. Many settled in Australia, Canada, Africa and the US, although recent years have seen families returning to the island.

Lithóstroto, Argostóli

Platía Valliánou (the central square) and the pedestrianised shopping street, Lithóstroto. The *platía* is at its liveliest during Carnival season, when a parade of *ármata* (floats) congregates here.

The Archaeological Museum

On Rókkou Vergóti, close to the theatre and opposite the beginning of Lithóstroto, is Argostóli's **Archaeological Museum** (usual hours Wed–Mon 8.30am–3.30pm, but currently closed for refurbishment; tel: 26710 28300). Three rooms contain a sizable collection of well-displayed pottery, jewellery, grave finds and statuary from prehistoric to late Classical times, offering a good overview of Kefaloniá's ancient history.

The first room has artefacts from the Palaeolithic period to the Bronze Age, as well as some interesting archive photos (1899–1933) of excavations on the island. The pieces on display range from very early flint hand tools (100,000–40,000 years old), to clay figurines (*c.*3rd century BC) from the cult centre of the Nymphs inside the Dhrákena Cave near Póros. The cave had been a settlement from late Neolithic times (8,000 BC onwards). Another case has finds (mostly *kantharoi*, or double-handled cups) from the Middle Helladic cist (box-shaped) graves (1750–1700 BC) and Mycenaean tholos (beehive) tombs at Kokoláta, just southeast of Argostóli.

Another room is devoted to finds from Mycenaean, or Mycenaean-influenced sites. By now the visitor will have noticed a certain grave and tomb theme to the exhibits. Perhaps the most important finds in this room come from the tholos tomb at Tzanáta near Póros. These include some delicately beaten gold, one piece of which shows the Mycenaean double-axe, clay figurines and an intriguing bronze buckle, indicating the existence of a powerful Mycenaean centre, probably related to Homeric Ithaca. It is thought that this will form vital evidence in pinpointing the exact location of the mythical kingdom.

The final room has displays of pieces from the Classical and Roman eras. There are a few larger exhibits, including a charming trident and dolphin floor mosaic from the 2nd-century BC sanctuary of Poseidon at Váltsa, on the Palikí Peninsula. The other cases mostly contain pieces from the four ancient cities of Kefaloniá (see page 15). Notable exhibits include an exquisite gold, winged Niké from Menegáta, a marble head of Silenos from Skinías village and a Roman 3rd-century AD bronze male head from Sámi.

The Korgialénios History and Folklore Museum

Up the hill, past the theatre, is the fascinating **Korgialénios History and Folklore Museum** ❸ (Ilía Zervoú 12; Mon 9am–noon, 6–9pm, Tue–Fri 9am–2pm, 6–9pm, Sat 10am–2pm; tel: 26710 28835), which is well worth a visit. Established after the 1953 earthquake to house objects salvaged from the

Ancient trade link

One of the most interesting exhibits in the Archaeological Museum is an Egyptian scarab from the reign of Thuthmose III (1479–1425 BC). It was found in the Mycenaean site at Krani, indicating trade links between Bronze-Age Kefaloniá and pharaonic Egypt.

View of Argostóli

wreckage, the museum provides a good overview of 19th-century Kefalonián domestic life. One refreshing aspect of the museum is its concentration on the lives and world of Kefalonián women, albeit mostly of the urban middle class. To this end, displays start with a case of household linen, as well as items such as kid gloves, silk stockings and hairpins. What follows is an amazing collection of urban women's costume between 1878 and 1910. These are displayed in replica period interiors, which give an excellent impression of the life of the Kefalonián upper class at the end of the 19th century.

For the most part, the dresses are highly elaborate and beautifully made in lace, silk and satin, with appliqué. There is a lovely pair of bridal shoes from 1905 and particularly exquisite is a young girl's ball gown of 1894, with silk tulle and embroidered roses. There are also a great number of accessories, including shawls, fans, parasols and gloves.

The museum also has a good display of pre-1953 Argostóli photographs. The earliest, from 1904–06 and taken by local photographer N. Trikardos, show it as a neat, provincial town. Some of the later (1930s) pictures were taken by two members of the Kosmetátou family. More disturbing are the images showing the total devastation of the town after the 1953 earthquake.

Other displays include a room with some rather dark, heavy furniture and portraits of local worthies, a lovely 18th-century carved and painted wooden iconostasis from the church of Ágios Geórgios, and a case with the personal effects of Dimitrios Korgialenios (died 1861), a member of the secret pro-independence Filikí Etería (Society of Friends). Finally, after a cluttered but cosy reconstruction of a traditional bedroom, there are displays of agricultural implements.

The Focás-Kosmetátou Foundation

Back towards the central *platía*, at Valliánou 1, stands a beautifully restored neo-classical mansion housing the **Focás-Kosmetátou Foundation** © (May–Oct Mon–Fri 10am–2pm, last admission 1.30pm; http://focas-cosmetatos.gr/main_en.html). The foundation, established in 1984 from the estate of three brothers, turned their family home into a museum to display their private collections

Ancient pottery on display at the Archaeological Museum

and to publish studies on Kefaloniá; it has also established the Votanókipos Kefaloniás on the outskirts of town (see page 35).

The museum part consists of just a single gallery with, to one side, a display of Greek numismatics and, opposite, a number of lithographs of the Ionian Islands and some pieces of furniture that belonged to the family. Of greatest interest are the lithographs by Joseph Cartwright, Edward Lear and Henry Cook, all of whom published volumes of paintings and engravings of the Ionians. Close by is a fine icon of Ágios Vikéndios (St Vincent of Zaragoza in the Catholic Church) attributed to Creto-Venetian master Theodoros Poulakis. Also look out for the 10 drachma bank note from the 1890s, cut in half; each half then became worth five drachmas. The small but pretty garden at the back is used to hold temporary exhibitions.

Lithóstroto and the Dhrápano Bridge

The main shopping street of Argostóli is the pedestrianised Lithóstroto, which runs south from Rókkou Vergóti, site of the town's theatre. Reconstructed after the 1953 earthquake, during the 19th and early-20th century this theatre, with its Italian opera productions, was the centre of social life for Argostóli's upper classes. Lithóstroto is lined with cafés, rivals to those in the central *platía*, and pricey clothing and shoe shops. About halfway down, at No. 42, is the town's bright yellow Catholic church of Ágios Nikólaos, serving the spiritual needs of the island's estimated 2,500 Catholic residents, plus visitors. Essentially rebuilt following the earthquake, its chief claim to fame is a

No-nonsense praise

'The buildings of Argostóli are handsome, and the town, though not remarkable for its liveliness, possesses many good streets and public edifices.'
Edward Lear, *Views in the Seven Ionian Islands*, 1863

Dhrápano Bridge

14th-century icon of Panagía Prevezána, enclosed in an ornate gold-painted frame. Beyond the church stands the **Pýrgos Kambánas** 🄳 (Kambána Tower), logically enough on Platía Kambánas. This reconstructed late 18th-century Venetian bell tower is no longer open to visitors, but there are cafés in the square where you can sit and watch the world go by.

From Platía Kambánas, head east/northeast towards the water along V. Vandhórou. Ahead of you, on the quay, stands the town's produce market. Depending on the season it may be piled high with all kinds of colourful agricultural produce.

Walking south along the waterfront brings you to the **Dhrápano Bridge** 🄴. This stone-built causeway crosses the shallow Koútavos Lagoon and was designed and built (first in wood) during 1812–13 by the French-Swiss Major Charles Philippe de Bosset. The stone structure in place today, supposedly the longest such structure in the world, dates from 1842, and has been

Column of light

On a short, manmade promontory off the tip of Cape Ágios Theódoros, northwest of Argostóli, stands a Doric-colonnaded lighthouse that originally dates from 1828. It was commissioned by Charles Napier, who served as the British Governor of Kefaloniá between 1822 and 1830. Destroyed by the 1953 earthquake, its present form is a reconstruction built in 1960.

repaired many times since. Out in the water near the end of the town, an obelisk erected by the townspeople in 1813 bears an inscription praising the supposed glories of the British Empire. In gratitude to the engineer, the British appointed De Bosset Governor of Kefaloniá until 1814.

The Katavóthres

Rizospastón heads north from central Platía Valliánou. On your right a short way up, at No. 12, you will pass Argostóli's **Filarmoniki Skholí** (Philharmonic School), and opposite, on the corner of the next block, the only building in town to have survived the 1953 earthquake intact. The perpendicular streets running off to the right lead down to the harbour.

Heading northwest along the quay, past the spot where you catch the ferry for Lixoúri, is a line of tavernas, best of which is Kyani Akti (see page 91). Before that, on the left, is a small square where, on a small patch of grass is the marble base of a Venetian fountain, with carved lions' heads. The column above it is of later (19th-century) provenance.

Continue along the coast, past a couple of pleasant tavernas and down a pine-shaded footpath beside the rocks, where local people swim in the evening. After about a kilometre (0.6 miles), you reach the tip of the cape. The views here over the mountains and the Argostóli Gulf are spectacular. Also here are the *Katavóthres* Ⓕ

The current at the Argostóli end was once strong enough in the past to drive the so-called sea-mills, built by the British to grind grain. After the 1953 earthquake the flow was disrupted and slowed to the gently running channels you see today. The original mill structures were destroyed in 1953 and replaced by a fake water wheel and a café, very popular with locals at Sunday midday. Further on, around the cape, are a series of small coves where you can swim.

Votanókipos Kefaloniás

Leaving town to the south, following Leofóros Yeoryíou Vergóti, brings you to a fork in the road. The left carries on to Peratáta, the right-hand turn has a signpost to the **Votanókipos Kefaloniás** Ⓖ (Cephalonia Botanica; May–Oct Mon–Sat 8.30am–2.30pm; www. focas-cosmetatos.gr; free). Follow the signs and don't be put off by the rough track, as it soon levels out. Bear left at the top of the rise and the site is 50m (160ft) along on your right.

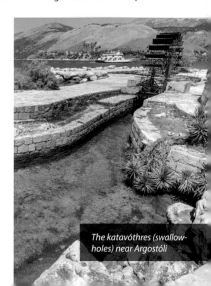

This botanical garden was established in 1998 by the Focás-Kosmetátou Foundation (see page 31) in an old olive grove. Its aim is to represent the rich flora of the different environments found on Kefaloniá, as well as seeking to preserve rare and endangered Kefalonián plants. The garden is affiliated to the Millennium

The katavóthres (swallow-holes) near Argostóli

Seed Bank coordinated by the Royal Botanic Gardens at Wakehurst, Sussex, in the UK. The site is beautiful and a world away from the nearby warehouses on the paved main road. An artificial stream runs through the centre of well laid-out and labelled areas, feeding an artificial lake that was created in 2008. During spring and early summer it is lovely to see the floor of the remaining olive grove carpeted with flowers, rather than the ploughed-up expanses usually glimpsed from the roadside.

THE LIVATHÓ AND SOUTH COAST

Southeast of Argostóli spreads the **Livathó Plain**, one of the few level areas on the island. Not surprisingly it is largely given over to agriculture. The road out of town bisects the plain, passing under the castle of Ágios Yeórgios above the villages of Peratáta and Mazarakáta (site of a Bronze Age necropolis), before, dominated by the bulk of Mount Énos to the east, it hugs the southern coast until the resort of Skála.

Ágios Geórgios Kástro

Towering above the plain is the Ágios Geórgios **Kástro ❷** (mid-June–Oct Wed–Mon 8.30am–3pm; free), continually being renovated and thus liable to unexpected closure. The fortress stands on a pine-clad hill, and can be reached from the north by the turn-off for the Orealios Gaea winery (see page 42) or via the twisty road from Peratáta. Either route brings you up to the Bórgo, the village outside the castle's walls. The view from the top is spectacular, and the Kastro Café outside the walls is a good place to take it in, particularly if you have just walked up in the heat and are in need of a light snack, dessert or a cold drink.

There has been a fortress on this site since Byzantine times, centred around the church of Ágios Geórgios from which the castle takes its name. In 1185 the island was taken by the Franks, and the kástro was controlled by them until 1485. After a brief period of Ottoman rule, the castle passed to the Venetians late in 1500 following a two-month siege. The fortifications seen today largely date from the period of Venetian occupation. At this time the castle was the centre of the island's administration. The town within mustered a population of 15,000 but in 1757 the Venetians moved their capital down to Argostóli, precipitating the fort's decline. Like all buildings in southern Kefaloniá, the castle suffered severe damage in the 1953 earthquake. However, it is well worth a visit – assuming you find it open – for the view and renovated walls.

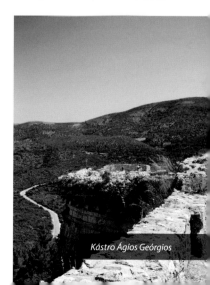

Kástro Ágios Geórgios

Back down in Peratáta, just beyond the village, is the turning for the monastery of

Agíou Andréou (also confusingly known as **Milapidiás**) ❸, now housed in modern (post-1953) buildings. Opposite these is the old church of Ágios Andréas, home to important 16th- to 18th-century icons by, among other masters, Emmanouil Lambardos (1590–1670) and Athanasios Anninos (1713–48). These are now part of the collection of the **Ecclesiastical Museum** (Mon–Sat 8am–2pm) housed within the church buildings. As well as good Ionian School paintings, the well-laid-out exhibits include reliquaries – one allegedly containing remains of Ágios Andréas himself – along with ecclesiastical vestments.

Lássi to Pessádha

A low but steep range of hills separates the Livathó Plain and Argostóli from the west coast. This hides some pretty villages, a couple of good wineries and, on the western side, attractive beaches. From Argostóli take either the main road out towards Lakíthra (then follow the signposts to the airport), or go around the cape via Ágios Theódoros and a number of bays, along a pleasant pine-flanked road. Both routes are walkable and will bring you to Lássi, the closest resort to Argostóli.

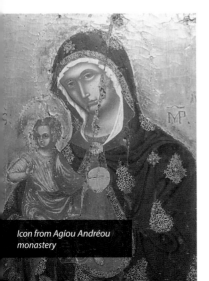

Icon from Agíou Andréou monastery

By Greek island standards **Lássi** ❹ is fairly low-key, although it does get crowded in high season. The

The beach at Lássi

star beaches here are **Makrýs** and **Platýs Gyalós**, both with fine sand and clean, blue water. The latter has a small island attached to the beach by a short isthmus. The coastal road continues south above cliffs with lovely views. After 2km (1.2 miles) you find the **Gentilini Winery** (tours and tastings daily May–Sept 11am–8pm, 1–20 Oct 10am–6.30pm; last entry for tours/tasting 1hr before closing; https://gentilini.gr). Owned by the Kosmetátou family, the winery was established in 1984 and specialises in high-quality organic wines, including a fine Robóla.

Beyond the Gentilini Winery and the airport is the pretty coastal village of Sarláta, topped by a rather Gothic, ivy-clad ruin. There are numerous rooms and villas to let here. Just along from Sarláta is **Domáta**, with houses spilling down the hillside.

The next village is **Metaxáta**, chiefly famous as the place where Byron stayed for four months in 1823 before leaving for Mesolóngi on the mainland, where he died. A bust of the poet can be seen in the main square, close to the site of the house where he stayed, which was later destroyed by the 1953 earthquake. Below Metaxáta and Domáta is **Kourkoumeláta**, close to the lovely beach of Ávythos. The attractive village was completely rebuilt by the four Vergotis brothers after 1953. At **Pessádha** ❺, where seasonal (May–Sept) ferries leave for Ágios Nikólaos on Zákynthos, **Divino Winery** (tours and tastings May–Oct daily 10am–6pm, Nov–Apr 10am–noon, 5–7pm; https://vinegarandroses.com) produces not only a dozen different wines but three types of vinegar, including one flavoured with Rosa celsiana, Damask rose.

Lourdháta to Skála

From the long beach at **Lourdháta**, well past Pessádha, to the village of Markópoulo there is little apart from ruined **Theotókou Sisíon monastery** which, as its name indicates, is believed to have been founded by St Francis of Assisi. The road southeast from here is fairly bleak, though towards the coast the land appears more fertile. After the right turn-off to Skála, the road rises towards **Markópoulo** ❻. The church and icon of Panagía Fidhoúsa here is the focus of a bizarre festival. Between the 7th and 15th of August hundreds of small, harmless snakes with a cross-shaped marking on their heads appear around the bell-tower, said to bring good luck to the village as well as to the many pilgrims who come to witness their arrival. Conversely, if these little snakes don't appear, difficult times lie ahead.

Taking the right-hand fork towards Skála takes you first past Káto **Kateliós**, and then the long sweep of sand of **Kamínia**. Before reaching Káto Kateliós you might want to call in at the **Metaxas Wine Estate** (May–Oct Mon–Fri 10.30am–2.30pm), actually best known for their production of Metaxa brandy, offered ubiquitously across Greece as a digestif. Káto Kateliós is a tiny, laid-back resort with a lovely sandy beach, on the opposite side of the bay from Kamínia. These two beaches are Kefaloniá's most important

Pebbled shoreline between Póros and Skála

nesting sites for loggerhead turtles, although far fewer nest here than on Zákynthos. Visitors should treat this area with respect and avoid the sand on mid-summer nights. In truth it shouldn't be necessary to disturb the turtles as just along the coast lies **Skála**, a popular, but relatively tasteful resort on a huge sandy beach backed by pine-clad hills. Also here, a little inland, are the excavated remains of a Roman villa (Wed–Mon 9am–4pm) with some vivid, well-preserved mosaic floors of the 3rd century AD.

MOUNT ÉNOS

The highest mountain in the Ionian Islands is **Mount Énos** ❼. At 1,632m (5,354ft) it dominates the southern part of Kefaloniá. Also still occasionally known by its Venetian name Monte Nero (the Black Mountain), its upper reaches are covered by Greek fir *(Abies cephalonica)*, giving the mountain a dark cap. The fir was

Goat on the flanks of Mount Énos

first identified on the island (hence its Latin name) and the Énos population is particularly important due to its lack of hybridisation. It is generally found at altitudes of between 800 and 1,600m (2,600–5,250ft) and grows up to 30m (100ft) tall. It was an important timber tree for the ancient Greeks, who used it extensively in shipbuilding, but is now strictly protected, with no logging allowed here.

Énos National Park

The indigenous population of firs is now protected by the **Énos National Park**. This takes in the slopes of Mount Énos above 1,000m (3,280ft) and the northern flanks of neighbouring Mount Roúdhi (also called Gioúpari; 1,124m/3,687ft). The two mountains are divided by a high saddle, which is marred by a NATO radar station bristling with satellite dishes. A tarmac road runs up to the saddle from the main road between Argostóli and Sámi. From the telecom masts it's another 1km (0.6 miles) downhill on an unpaved road to a slightly wider stretch where you can park (be warned it is rough going, and don't be tempted to drive any further than this point). A signposted footpath ascends to the summit, Mégas Sorós. If it is not too hazy the views from the top are incomparable.

The turn-off towards Valsamáta will take you to Orealios Gaea Wine Cooperative ❽ (formerly the **Cephalonian Robola Producers Cooperative)** at Frangáta (tastings all year daily

9am–6pm; www.orealios.gr). The Robóla grape is cultivated on the high altitude limestone soils found in the region and is used to produce a fine white wine. The cooperative makes a dozen or more wines per year, including some good reds and rosé.

Close to the winery, just beyond Valsamáta, is the monastery of **Agíou Gerasímou** ❾ (daily 9am–1pm and 3.30–8pm, but call in advance to confirm; tel: 26710 86385). Ágios Gerásimos (1509–1570), although born on the Peloponnese, has become the patron saint of Kefaloniá, and the convent, founded in the 16th century, is the most important pilgrimage site on the island. The (male) saint founded a female order in 1554 and was beatified in 1622; his festival days are 16 August and 20 October.

Focus of the new convent church, consecrated in 1992, is the saint's silver shrine, inside of which is the reliquary containing his supposedly uncorrupted remains; his funeral robes are draped over the shrine. Although the church is modern, it still contains many fine original works of art, as well as a staircase that descends to a couple of small chambers, thought to be the saint's meditation sanctuary.

If you're feeling hungry after your devotions at the monastery, between there and Valsamáta village awaits an excellent meat-focused taverna, Botsolos (see page 92).

SÁMI AND PÓROS

The road from Argostóli over the flanks of Mount Énos descends past fir-clad slopes to the small port of **Sámi**. Ferries leave from here for the island of Itháki, and for Pátra on the mainland. Sámi

Feral ponies

The semi-wild ponies of Mount Énos are descended from animals abandoned after World War II. They initially formed communities of up to 100 animals but are now highly endangered, numbering only some 12–14 individuals. If you are lucky enough to spot them, be careful not to disturb them.

is a pleasant, quiet town with a few eating places along the harbourfront. This town was the location for much of the filming of *Captain Corelli's Mandolin* in 2000 (see page 47). For the filming, much of Sámi's pre-earthquake architecture was reconstructed as a set, only to be destroyed during the subsequent battle scenes.

East over the headland of Cape Dhihália (also known as Mýtikas) is the beautiful white shingle beach of **Andísamos** ⑩, also used as a location for the film. Surrounded by steep, maquis-clad hills, the deep inlet looks out on the southern coast of Itháki. The clear water is great for swimming; the furthest little cove of the beach is nudist.

The Dhrogaráti and Melissáni Caves

On the road from Argostóli, about 3km (2 miles) before Sámi, is the turning for the **Dhrogaráti Cave** ⑪ (Apr–Oct daily 9am–7pm, sometimes later in peak season). The cave was discovered about 300 years ago, after an earthquake opened up the present entrance. A steep series of steps leads down into a cool fissure, at the bottom of which a concrete viewing platform overlooks the huge chamber. Occasionally used to hold concerts, it has an impressive array of stalactites. Some of these are damaged, broken off by unthinking souvenir hunters, but there is still a huge amount of flowstone remaining. From the platform you can make your way down on to the floor of the chamber, where you can explore the nooks and crannies. To see the chamber at its best, wait until the tour groups have departed, when you can explore on your own.

Perhaps even more impressive is the cave-lake at **Melissáni** ⑫ (May–Oct daily 9am–7pm, Nov–Apr variable hours; https://kefaloniageopark.gr/en/node/302), west of Sámi by the little resort of Karavómylos. A short artificial tunnel brings you to the edge of a large underground lake, partly open to the sky due to the collapse of the cavern's roof; the sunlight on the deep, clear water turns it an iridescent blue. Visitors are rowed around the lake by waiting boatmen.

Exploring Dhrogaráti Cave

The cave was formed between 20,000 and 16,000 years ago, during the last ice age. The roof of the cavern collapsed some 5,000 years ago; the debris from this event still lies in the centre of the lake. Perhaps the most fascinating aspect of its geology is that it is the point of re-emergence for the water that sinks at the katavóthres near Argostóli, hence the water in the cave is brackish. It enters the lake at its deepest point (32m/104ft) on the left-hand side, and sinks again at the far point of the covered section of the cave which lies to your right.

It was in the still-intact section of the cavern that archaeological finds were made, dating from the 4th–3rd century BC, confirming that the cave had been the site of a cult of Pan and the Nymphs.

From Karavómylos, the coast road runs north around the bay of Sámi, to the small port of **Agía Evfimía** ⓫ (Agia-Thymiá in the local dialect). This attractive yachting harbour has a great location, with steep, bare mountainsides looming behind and a sweeping view

Looking out over Póros

east over the water to Itháki. The town's narrow shingle beach, north of the yachting harbour – now backed by rather stark concrete seawalls – has wonderfully clear water and the swimming here is excellent.

Póros

The main road south from Sámi passes through some beautiful countryside, as well as the attractive mountain villages of Dhigaléto and Ágios Nikólaos, which are close to the **Ávythos Lake**, not to be confused with the eponymous beach near the airport. Just beyond Ágios Nikólaos, on the hairpin bends, are the ruins of a monastery. From here the road runs straight down to the village of Tzanáta.

Tzanáta lies in a fertile bowl. On a small rise in the vale is a Mycenaean tholos (beehive) tomb, excavated in 1992–94. The earliest finds date from *c.*1350 BC and the high quality of the artefacts – including jewellery, pottery and seals – points to the existence of a powerful Mycenaean centre. It is thought that this may identify Tzanáta as the location of Homeric Ithaca.

Between Tzanáta and Póros the road passes through the short but impressive 80m (260ft) -deep **Póros Gorge**, the channel for a seasonal river. The town of **Póros** ⑭ is divided by a rocky headland, on the far side of which is the port and fishing harbour. Ferries sail from here to Kyllíni on the mainland. As a resort, one of the first developed on Kefaloniá, Póros has a quiet, seen-better-days air. That said, the 2km (1.2mile) -long pebbly town beach has very clear waters and there are some nice secluded, rocky bays around the southerly headland.

CAPTAIN CORELLI'S MANDOLIN

This novel, by the British author Louis de Bernières and set in Kefaloniá during World War II, was first published in 1994 and became a bestseller through word of mouth. The book concerns the exploits of Antonio Corelli, a mandolin-playing captain in the occupying Italian army, and Pelagia, daughter of the local doctor. The core of the text is their love story but this is also set against the German takeover of September 1943, after the capitulation of the Italians, and the subsequent massacre of Italian troops, and any islander found helping them, by the German army. Add in the Greek communist resistance, a ridiculous upper-class English intelligence officer who can only speak ancient Greek and a film tie-in starring Nicolas Cage and Penélope Cruz, shot on location on Kefaloniá, and you have the Captain Corelli phenomenon.

Although the book has been an international success with the reading public, it has stirred up the passions of locals and historians alike. Their major objection is the book's portrayal of the Leftist resistance (known by the acronym ΕΛΑΣ or ELAS). Well-loved and regarded as national heroes by many Greeks – and aided in this case after 1943 by Italian fighters – its portrayal in the book is suspect. The strong anti-communist – and historically inaccurate – bias to the text defames not only the movement as a whole, but, more specifically, the partisan Amos Pampaloni on whose life and memoirs it seems to have been based. Pampaloni fought with Greek partisans both on Kefaloniá and on the mainland and he objected strongly to this historical distortion while he was alive.

To the north of town is the long, excellent beach of Rágia, above which is the **Theotókou Átrou monastery** (take the right turn just after the gorge on leaving town). This is said to be the longest established monastery on Kefaloniá, first mentioned in 1264, though obviously much rebuilt since. The beautiful road south to Skála follows the deserted coastline. Some 3km before reaching Skála, next to the little chapel of Ágios Geórgios, lie the remains of an Archaic (6th-century BC) temple to Apollo.

THE PALIKÍ PENINSULA

On the opposite (western) side of the gulf from Argostóli juts out the large Palikí Peninsula (also known as the Lixoúri Peninsula), which, away from its south coast, is barely touched by tourism. On the east coast lies its major town, Argostóli's traditional rival Lixoúri.

Lixoúri

Easily reached by an hourly ferry, **Lixoúri** now plays second fiddle to Argostóli and is a sleepy, laid-back place. However, it's worth taking the ferry, which takes around 20 minutes, for the views of the gulf alone and there are a few sights worth seeing in the town. It is also a good jumping-off point for other places on the peninsula.

Lixoúri developed under Venetian rule (becoming officially recognised in 1534), but about 1.5km (1 mile) north of town is the site of ancient Pali, one of the four ancient city- states of the island (see page 15). Much of Lixoúri was destroyed in 1953 but a few major buildings have been reconstructed as before. The earliest of these is the colonnaded Markáto, just behind the seafront where the Argostóli ferry docks. It was built in 1824 by British governor, Charles Napier, served as Kefaloniá's first courtroom, but now houses the local Citizens' Advice Bureau (ΚΕΠ in Greek). Many of Lixoúri's buildings suffered further damage in the January 2014 earthquake.

Further along, on the corner of Grígóri Lambráki and Skarlátou, is the **Filarmonikí Skholí** (Philharmonic School), occupying a fine neoclassical building originally dating from 1836, but rebuilt in 1963. There are four such 'schools' – wind and brass ensembles, probably a legacy of British rule – on the island: here, in Argostóli, and in Sámi and Póros. Wind instruments, including the flute of founder Petros Skarlatos (1820–1904), are on show in the prettily decorated first-floor rehearsal room.

Also in the town, up the hill on Ekaterínis (from the port walk up Pávlou Dhellapórta, then Mihaïl Avílhou) is the **Iakovatios Museum and Library** (closed since the 2014 earthquake). The attractive 1866 neoclassical building and its shady garden were donated to the Greek state by the prominent Tipaldos-Iakovatos family in 1963, along with a library of around 25,000 volumes, a few dating back to the late 16th century. The attached museum has 18th- and 19th-century ecclesiastical vestments, plus heirlooms of the donor family, including period furniture, icons, three early gospels, portraits of notable Kefaloniáns and a small archaeological collection

On the waterfront is a statue of local satirical writer and poet Andreas Laskaratos (1811–1901), his back turned on Argostóli across the water. For his alleged impiety he was excommunicated by the local bishop, which meant that he would not decay in his grave and ran the risk of becoming a vampire; in response, he asked the cleric to

Steady as a rock

Just along from Xí beach lies Kounópetra beach, named for its Kounópetra (rocking stone). This flat slab of stone used to rock in the waves, but the 1953 earthquake disturbed its balance, so that it no longer moves.

excommunicate his favourite pair of boots, so that they too would remain incorruptible in perpetuity. By way of contrast, the Venetian-educated religious polemicist – and later bishop on the Peloponnese – Ilias Miniates (1669–1714) was also born here.

The south and east coasts

South of Lixoúri spreads the plain of Katogí, the most fertile area on the island, planted with wheat and vines. This suffered greatly in the 1953 earthquake and the effect on the now-fractured topography is obvious. The southern coast has some lovely beaches; the most popular and spectacular are the orange-sand stretches of **Mégas Lákkos** and its continuation, **Xí** ⓱.

North of Xí is the village of Mantzavináta, unremarkable except for the **Vitoratos Winery** (summer daily 10am–2pm, 6–8pm; book tours on 26710 94244). Beyond Matzavináta to the west is **Havriáta**, the location of one of the first schools on the island, founded by the 18th-century philosopher Vikentios Damados (1700–52).

Back towards Lixoúri, at **Soullári**, the church of Agía Marína dates from 1600 and contains icons by the Creto-Venetian master-painters Immanouil Moskhos and Theodoros Poulakis.

North of town, past the port of ancient Pali at modern Karavostási, awaits the monastery of Panagías **Kehriónos** ⓲. Its church is currently closed due to damage caused by the 2014 earthquake, although an annual festival may still be held outside on 23 August. Some 5km (3 miles) further on awaits the small but important wetland area of Harboúri ⓳, just inland from the beach near the village of **Livádhi**.

Anogí

The mountainous northern and western part of the peninsula is known as Anogí. Towards the southern end of the wild and deserted west coast stands the **monastery of Theotókou Kypouréon** , founded in 1759 by three local sailors, imprisoned in Algiers, who prayed successfully to the Panagía for their liberation; perched high on cliffs, this can be a spectacular place to watch the sunset. Below lurks the sea-cave of **Dhrakospilía** (Dragon's Cave). A spring at the ruined nearby church of Agía Paraskeví is said to cure stomach ailments. Some 10km (6 miles) up the coast as the crow flies – but longer via the roads which twist along just inland – is undoubtedly the finest beach on the peninsula, **Petaní** ㉑, a beautiful stretch of pebbles backed by steep cliffs – and two tavernas, of which Xouras (see page 92) is recommended.

Xí beach

Before reaching Petaní you pass through the village of **Kondogenádha**. In addition to its restored 18th- and 19th-century vernacular architecture, the village is home to two important churches, the 12th–to–13th-century Ágios Geórgios and Ágios Ioánnis Theológos, with an impressive carved iconostasis.

THE NORTH

The north of Kefaloniá escaped the worst ravages of the 1953 earthquake and thus retains a substantial amount of traditional architecture. The landscape is barren and spectacularly steep, particularly along the **west coast road**, which offers the best, if most alarming, ride on the island.

Northwest coast villages

From Argostóli the road takes you past the turning for the village of **Dhavgáta ㉒**, the location of the **Museum of Natural History** (June–Sept daily 9am–3pm, Oct–May Mon–Fri 9am–3pm). Set up primarily as an educational centre and library, it provides a useful introduction to local geology, flora and fauna.

The coast road continues to Fársa, where it starts to climb. Just inland huddles the old village, ruined in 1953. Below, and along this whole stretch of coast, you see rows of fish farms. Beyond Angónas the view along the northwest coast opens up – a steep line of cliffs falling into blue sea. Down to the west are the beaches of **Agía Kyriakí ㉓** and **Voúti**. The long, exposed stretch of sand at Agía Kyriakí can attract flotsam but the small pebbly bay at Voúti, reached down

Picturesque prison

Dating from the late 16th century, the fortress at Ássos was used as a prison until 1953. Prisoners tended the vines that covered the hillsides and clifftops above Ássos village.

View of Ássos

a quite rough dirt road from the village of Zóla, is cleaner, with a single kantína and sunbeds for hire. It can get very warm here, even in early summer.

From here onward the sharp hairpins of the road hug the cliff edges. This is Kefaloniá's equivalent of fabled oceanside Highway 1 in California. The views – back to the largely inaccessible north coast of Palikí and forward to Ássos – are wonderful.

Mýrtos and Ássos

Some 10km (6 miles) beyond Angónas the road turns sharply inland, forming a large hairpin around the truly spectacular bay of **Mýrtos** ㉔. The best place to see the beach and cliffs is from the lay-by on the main road on the northern side of the bay. Looking down, you see a crescent of bright white beach bordered by the cornflower blue of the sea and surrounded by sheer cliffs. The way down to the beach is via the steep but well-paved road from

Dhivaráta. Once there, it does not quite live up to its view from above. What appeared to be white sand turns out to be small pebbles, and it can get very busy. The beach also feels too organised, with sunbeds, a café and lifeguards – essential, as the sea can be dangerous here, with strong lateral currents and an undertow.

From Dhivaráta a road continues east (bear left before the village to go north). The inland road crosses the island, through a gap in the mountains, to the attractive coastal village of Agía Evfimía (see page 45), passing on the way a couple of derelict Venetian windmills that were previously used for pumping water up from wells.

The road north from Dhivaráta and **Mýrtos** carries on in a similarly spectacular fashion. About 3km (2 miles) after a viewpoint layby is the steep descent to **Ássos** ㉕. At the bottom is Ássos village, with its charming natural harbour. The village retains much of its traditional architecture (reconstructed with the help of the City of Paris, commemorated by a plaque in Platía Parisíon), and in spring and early summer is covered in flowers. The small beach in the harbour is fairly clean, but just round the coast are some beautiful coves that are only accessible by boat.

Connected to the village by a short isthmus is an enormous Venetian *kástro* (fortress) on top of a hill. Begun in 1593, it served to protect the Venetian fleet and island from attack by Ottomans and pirates alike. In more recent history it was used as a prison (see box, page 52). The winding path up to it takes you up through pine woods and gives fine views over the harbour and neighbouring coast. Apart from the walls and the lovely curving entrance, little remains inside, although a visitors' centre has been sensitively built in the middle.

Around Fiskárdho

The road beyond Ássos ends up at the harbour of Fiskárdho at the northeastern tip of the island. This is perhaps the most immediately attractive part of Kefaloniá, with much surviving traditional vernacular architecture. Two of the most attractive **hill villages** here are **Vasilikiádes**, on the main road 10km (6 miles) before Fiskárdho, and nearby **Mesovoúnia**. The latter is on the easterly road to Agía Evfimía. This passes through a succession of very pretty mountain villages – **Varý**, **Karyá** and **Komitáta** – and the views over to the neighbouring island of Itháki are magnificent. The only sounds across this landscape, with its dry stone walls and abandoned stone houses, are the tinkling of cow and goat bells. Water is at a premium here, and there are numerous rainwater cisterns with concrete paved catchments just above. The view down to Agía Evfimía from Komitáta is breathtaking.

Towards Fiskárdho itself on the easiest road you pass through **Mánganos**, with its excellent greengrocer, full of wonderful local

The bay of Mýrtos

Fiskárdho harbour

fruit and vegetables, plus olives, oil and wine, and **Andipáta Erísou**, at the turn-off for **Dhafnoúdi beach** (see page 57). **Fiskárdho** itself survived the 1953 earthquake intact, and has cashed in on this with a vengeance. The admittedly very attractive harbourfront is backed by pastel-shaded housing, now largely expensive restaurants, cafés and boutiques. The harbour, for better or worse, is also greatly beloved by yachters, particularly those on flotilla holidays (it can be fun to sit on the quayside watching novice sailors try to bring their boats in for mooring).

The port, thought to be the location of ancient Panormos, takes its modern name from Robert Guiscard, a Norman soldier/adventurer who died here in 1085 after spending most of his martial career in what is now Italy, although he is buried back in Normandy. There is also a Roman cemetery (2nd–4th centuries AD). Towards the Venetian lighthouse, on the northern headland, stands an interesting church, started by the Byzantines, but largely Norman in execution (c.12th century). At the southern end of the harbour, the former school houses the **Nautical and Environmental Museum** (summer Mon–Sat 10am–6pm, Sun 10am–2pm; tel: 26710 41081; donations encouraged), run by volunteers from the FNEC (Fiskárdho Nautical and Environmental Club) European exchange programme. Exhibits in its single room include the skeleton of a Cuvier's beaked whale, found dead on nearby Émblysi beach in 1995, as well as displays describing local birds and mammals and their habitats.

The northern coast has some wonderful small and quiet **beaches**, all of which have the clearest imaginable water. Some of the most idyllic little bays, with their white pebble beaches, are only accessible by boat (easily hired for the day in Fiskárdho, see page 66). The two most easily accessible from Fiskárdho are, immediately to the north, **Émblysi** and, to the south, the beautiful bay of **Fóki**. Heavenly **Dhafnoúdi** meanwhile is reached by a 20-minute walk down through the pine trees from the village of Andipáta Erísou. Tiny **Alatiés**, southwest of Mánganos village, lies tucked between folds of impressive white volcanic rock), but nearby sand-and-gravel **Agía Ierousalím**  beyond Halikerí hamlet surpasses all of the

Shopping lane in Fiskárdho

preceding, and has one of the best and friendliest tavernas on the island, Odysseas (see page 93).

ITHÁKI

Easily visited from Kefaloniá, the rugged island of Itháki has a history that's intimately tied up with that of its larger neighbour. Claimed by many, particularly the locals, to be the mythical homeland of the Homeric hero Odysseus, there is little archaeological evidence to support this claim (indeed, it seems as though Homeric Ithaca is likely to lie close to present-day Póros on Kefaloniá, see page 46). Homer wrote of Odysseus's homeland: 'There are no tracks, nor grasslands . . . it is a rocky, severe island, unsuited for horses, but not so wretched, despite its small size. It is good for goats.' The modern island still fits that description to perfection. Daily ferries leave from Sámi on Kefaloniá and dock at the tiny harbour of Písaetós on the west coast of Itháki.

Vathý harbour, Itháki

Like Kefaloniá, Itháki suffered greatly from the 1953 earthquake, causing many people to emigrate (the population dropped from around 15,000 to under 3,000). However, it is a supremely beautiful and unspoilt island with a lovely main town, Vathý, and some gorgeous, largely deserted, pebble beaches.

VATHÝ AND THE NORTH

Vathý ㉙ lies on the island's east coast, at the head of a deep, southeast-pointing bay on the larger Mólos Gulf. It is a quiet, very attractive town (it still retains surviving pre-earthquake architecture, while damage was assiduously repaired in traditional style) with a number of tavernas set around its harbourfront and an **Archaeological Museum** (usual hours Wed–Mon 8.30am–3.30pm, but currently closed for renovation; tel: 26740 32200). Ferries depart for Astakós on the central mainland during peak season only; otherwise all services call at Pisaetós port.

To the north, the road crosses the isthmus and either heads up to the mountain-top village of Anogí or along the western coast through Léfki. **Anogí**, only occupied for half the year, has fabulous views as well as the Byzantine church of Kímisis tis Theotókou. Before reaching Léfki you pass above a series of small, quiet pebble beaches: Vrýsi, Áspros Gialós, Komninoú Ámmos and Koutoúpi.

The roads through both Léfki and Anogí join at **Stavrós**, the island's second-largest town. This sits above the small ancient port of Polis (a 20-minute walk). There is a small **Archaeological Museum** (Wed–Mon 8.30am–3.30pm) here, housing local finds. These mostly come from the early Bronze Age site at nearby Pelikáta, one of the many sites – with roads, walls and other structures – claimed as the location of the palace of Odysseus.

North of Stavrós a road winds up to the hill village of Exogí. On the way up is an excavation known as the School of Homer, in reality a tower dating from the 6th century BC; close by is a Mycenaean

Twin peaks

IthÁki is essentially two groups of mountains linked by a narrow isthmus. On the eastern side of the isthmus is the deep Mólos Gulf, while on the north coast is the large bay of Afáles, one of several.

tomb. Below, reached from the hamlet of Platithriés, is the spectacular bay of **Afáles** ㉚ with its lovely beach. From the beach at Afáles a rough but beautiful minor road heads north towards Cape Dhrákou Pídhima (Dragon's Leap), before doubling back south along the northeast coast to the isolated white-pebble beach at Mármakas ㉛, more usually reached from Fríkes.

After the quiet port of Fríkes on the northeast coast, a favourite yachting harbour and one terminus of seasonal ferry service to Lefkádha island (often via Fiskárdho), the main road heads east to **Kióni** ㉜, an attractive place and Ithàki's most upmarket resort. Like Fiskárdho on Kefaloniá, Kióni survived the 1953 earthquake mostly undamaged, and has capitalised on this in a similar fashion, something evident in the prices for accommodation. The coast between Fríkes and Kióni has a number of attractive peb-

bly beaches, accessible by road or on foot. The walk up to Anogí from Kióni, along a clearly marked path, is delightful and takes around 1.5 hours each way. Beyond Anogí stands the monastery of Panagía Katharón, with its wonder-working icon discovered by peasants clearing nearby scrubland. The 8 September festival here sees a procession and music after the liturgy.

THE ODYSSEUS TRAIL

The south of the island has a number of sites that

Itháki's main town, Vathý

are supposedly linked with events in Homer's *The Odyssey* (see page 17). Close to Vathý, up the hill from the beach at Dhexá (identified as ancient Phorkys, the landing place of Odysseus), is the **Cave of the Nymphs (Marmarospíli)** ㉝. This spot is supposedly where the Greek hero, helped by the goddess Athene, hid the cauldrons, tripods, cloaks and cups given to him by the Phaeakian king, Alkinous.

Statue of Odysseus

Odysseus, transformed by the goddess into an old man, met up with Eumaeus (his old palace swineherd) at the **Arethoúsa Spring** ㉞, where the pigs were being watered. The spring is in the south of the island, 3km (2 miles) from Vathý (a 3hr round-hike), along a steep but well-marked path (look for splashes of green paint). Above the spring yawns the Cave of Eumaeus, and the crag known as Kórax (the raven), which matches Homer's description.

On the other side of the island, towards the harbour and pebble beach at **Pisaetós**, is the Archaic-era site of **Alalkomenae** ㉟ (*c.*700 BC), which can be reached by taxi or rented scooter. This was wrongly identified by German archaeologist Heinrich Schliemann in 1878 as the palace of Odysseus, where the hero came back to win back his wife, Penelope, from her suitors.

Above Písaetós, well back towards Vathý, looms the village of **Perahóri**, close to the island's now deserted, ruined medieval capital, Paleohóra.

The crystal clear waters of
Agia Paraskevi beach

THINGS TO DO

SPORTS

The wonderfully clear sea and spectacular mountains of Kefaloniá invite visitors to do more than just sit in a deck chair looking out at the view. Options for active holidays are numerous, from swimming, diving and sailing to walking, cycling and horse riding.

WATER SPORTS

Swimming. The water quality around the islands is excellent. The water is extremely clear and clean and, in general, safe; though be careful at some of the west-facing beaches, particularly Mýrtos on Kefaloniá, as there can be some very nasty undercurrents. For little children, the southern and eastern beaches of Zákynthos (for example Kalamáki, Pórto Koúkla and Tsiliví) are best, as they have gently sloping sand and calm waters. Otherwise, most hotels and many apartments have swimming pools, though in summer it would be a shame not to take advantage of the warm waters surrounding the islands. At some points (notably the pebbly beaches around the north and eastern coasts of Kefaloniá) the view from the water over to Itháki or Lefkáda is stunning.

Boat hire

Hiring a small (25 horsepower) motorboat is the best way to explore secluded and otherwise inaccessible bays. Boats are available from outlets in many places on Kefaloniá, and cost €50–100 per day plus petrol. They are great for swimming from – simply anchor, then dive or jump off the side; all boats have a fold-down ladder to help you get back on board.

Hiker at the top of Mount Enos

Snorkelling and diving. The coasts around Zákynthos and Kefaloniá are a divers' paradise – the rocky shoreline is home to wide variety of creatures, and the calm, clear water gives visibility up to 50m (165ft). All scuba-diving schools have qualified instructors who will choose dive locations according to your experience. Extended boat trips are available for advanced divers. For the more advanced trips, or to hire equipment and go by yourself, you will need to show a diving certificate. Most major resorts have reputable diving schools. Well-reputed dive centres approved by the Professional Association of Diving Instructors (PADI; www.padi. com) include Diving Center Turtle Beach at Límni Kerioú (tel: 26950 49424; www.diving-center-turtle-beach.com), on Zákynthos, and Aquatic World in Agía Evfimía (tel: 26740 62006; www.aquatic.gr), on Kefaloniá. If you don't want to indulge in full-scale scuba diving, snorkelling with simply a mask, snorkel and flippers can be equally rewarding.

WALKING

The islands not only have wonderful coasts but also beautiful interiors, much of them mountainous. There is some superb walking here and not all of it strenuous. The goal of more serious hikers will be the summit of Mount Énos (the highest peak in the Ionians), best tackled from the saddle between it and Mount Roúdi. There are companies that conduct walking tours of the islands, for interesting trips to Kefaloniá contact Trek Adventures (tel: 01789 868002; www.trek-adventures.co.uk). Serious botanists will find the hills of the islands a delight, and there are tailor-made botanical walking holidays available.

HORSE RIDING AND BICYCLING

These are both excellent ways of seeing Kefaloniá. In Koulouráta, about 6km (4 miles) south of Sámi, the Bavarian Horse Riding Stables (www.kephalonia.com/bavarian-horse-riding-stables),

YACHTING

The relatively calm and safe waters around Zákynthos and Kefaloniá, coupled with the wonderful marine environment, have made this area very popular with yacht owners and companies running bareboat charter and flotilla holidays. On Kefaloniá the most popular harbour is Fiskárdho in the north of the island. However, this can get very busy, especially with novice crews being instructed through loudhailers by their group leader on the quayside. If you are after a little more peace and quiet then you would be better advised to head down the coast to Agía Evfimía or along the spectacular west coast to the pretty horseshoe harbour of Ássos. Companies that charter boats and run flotillas include Sunsail (www.sunsail.com) and Nautilus (www.nautilusyachting.com).

with more than a dozen well-cared-for horses, offers outings from one hour to two days on horseback, mostly through the mountains but also one route along the coast; prices range from €30 for the shortest rides, up to €250 (bed and board included) for two full days in spring or autumn only.

The mountainous nature of the terrain makes cycling hard work but extremely rewarding. Many of the minor roads are very quiet but take great care on the precipitous main coast roads. In the UK, Trek Adventures (https://trek-adventures.co.uk/cycling-bike-hire) can organise cycling expeditions in advance, based at accommodation on the flattish Palikí Peninsula, as well as a steep climb up Mount Énos from Argostóli. On Kefaloniá itself, contact Rent a Bike Kefaloniá at Stamatíou Pylarinoú 1, Argostóli (tel: 26710 26602; www.rentabikekefalonia.gr), April to mid-Oct only. Alternatively, try Ainos Bike and Scooter Rent Kefaloniá at Sitempóron 61–63, cnr. V. Vandhórou (tel: 26710 26874; www.ainosbikes.com).

Cyclists

EXCURSIONS BY KAÏKI OR RENTED SMALL BOAT

The best Kefalonián boat excursions start from Agía Evfimía. Heading south towards Sámi, you may call at the otherwise hard-to-access beaches at Agía Paraskeví (pebbly, with a taverna); Karavómylos (again pebbly, with a taverna); and a rare sandy beach just before Sámi. Heading north towards Fiskárdho, choose from among (in this order) Roboli Bay; Giagana, with trees almost down to the water; Horgota, used as a filming location for Captain Corelli's Mandolin; and finally the double beach of Agía Sofía (with a seasonal kantína), which is probably as far as you can safely get from your start point on a typical tank of fuel. Small boats can be hired from Yellow Boats (tel: 6937 571950; http://yellowboats-kefalonia.gr) in Agía Evfimía.

In Fiskárdho, a craft rented from Regina's Boats (tel: 6938 984647; https://fiscardoboatrental.com) will allow you easy access to all the small, remote coves along the northern coast (see page 54).

HIKING

Kefaloniá is not really a walkers' paradise – too many roads, too much private land. The premier excursion is to the summit of Mount Énos, with a marked trail from the end of the road up the mountain.

ENVIRONMENTAL VOLUNTEERS

One of the most satisfying ways of seeing Kefaloniá is to volunteer on an environmental protection programme run by a local eco-groups.

Visitors under 25 years of age can apply to take part in one of the programmes run by the FNEC (Fiskárdho Nautical and Environmental Club), based at the Nautical and Environmental Museum (see page 56). As well as carrying out marine research work, it also co-ordinates a network of volunteers to protect the feral ponies on Mount Énos.

SHOPPING

Prices are steadily rising in Greece, and as a result you shouldn't expect great bargains on Kefaloniá. In souvenir and gift shops you might find that some good-natured bargaining is tolerated if you are buying more than one item or spending a reasonable amount, but don't push your luck. Local profit margins have to cover not only the tourist months but also the off season, when most shops are closed.

If you are not a resident of the EU, you might be able to claim back the 23 percent VAT (sales tax) included in the price of most goods, if you spend over a certain amount. Ask for details at any shops with 'Tax-Free for Tourists' stickers.

WHAT TO BUY

Truth be told, Kefaloniá is not a shoppers' paradise and the best things to buy as gifts or mementos of your trip are perishables, such as olive oil, thyme honey and local wines (see page 83).

Shop in Fiskárdho

Among the tourist merchandise peddled in the resorts, from inflatable sea-creatures and novelty key rings, you'll have to look hard to find anything worth bringing home. An exception to this is jewellery, in gold and silver, which can be of very good quality and made in attractive, unusual designs. In Argostóli most of the jewellers are along Lithóstroto. Note that the more upmarket the resort (for example, Fiskárdho), the more inflated the price of the jewellery is likely to be.

Another item worth looking out for is a decent reproduction icon. These can be skilfully executed and are widely available, but the best ones tend to be on sale at monasteries.

Leather items, especially bags and sandals, can be good buys but you might want to shop around for the best quality and selection.

Ceramics are among the few artisanal items worth bringing home. The following outlets on Kefaloniá are worth sampling. In Lássi, Stella Komina (tel: 26710 24016; https://ceramicskefalonia. wixsite.com/stellakomina) has one of the largest pottery workshops on the island. The IN Gallery in Sámi (tel: 26740 22883; https://ingallerykefalonia.com) sells paintings and other works from local artists, as well as pottery.

Olive-wood articles make another excellent souvenir or gift purchase – you will typically find salad sets, spatulas, napkin rings, bowls, platters and chopping boards in every imaginable size. Go for one-piece chopping boards, over glued items, as these will soon come apart if immersed in water. If taken care of, with regular oiling, such articles can last a lifetime. Sadly, many craftsmen prefer to work with softer, green, uncured wood, which tends to develop cracks as it continues drying at home. The workshop of Kostas Annikas Deftereos in Sámi (tel: 6938 762384; www.annikas. gr) is recommended; he also carries a selection of pottery, plus items made from beech, poplar and walnut wood.

NIGHTLIFE

Nightlife on Kefaloniá ranges from the more traditionally Greek, particularly authentic renditions of *kandádes*, the Italianate, melodic song form of the Ionian islands accompanied by guitar and mandolin (see page 14), to the heavily tourist-orientated ('Greek nights') in the most commercial tavernas and larger resort hotels. There is also nightlife to be found around the handful of bars in the beach resorts of Lássi and Skála. Argostóli can offer two proper clubs: Bass on Platía Valliánou, and Katavothres, out at the eponymous geological phenomenon, housed in a historic 1950s building designed by seminal architect Aris Konstantinides.

GREEK NIGHTS

Whichever resort you choose to stay in on Kefaloniá, you will almost certainly come across a 'Greek Night', which generally comprises a passably traditional meal, music (usually live) and dancing. It is, of course, the last that everyone comes to see. Traditional Greek dances are taught at an early age, and the dancers – be they specially hired performers, restaurant staff or simply locals who want to do their bit – can almost always be relied on for an energetic performance.

Whereas some Greek island dances are a little staid, Kefalonián males revel in athletic, fast dances with high-kicking, Cossack-like steps and not a little bravado. Dancing in a ring of fire is quite typical. Another dance involves picking up a glass of wine with the mouth (no hands allowed) from a press-up position. The wine is downed with a jerk of the neck. Another crowd pleaser is the solo *zeïbékiko*, traditionally a male preserve but now performed by women too. The spectators, clapping in time to the music, cheer on the dance. By the end of the night, it is a fair bet that the dancers will have cajoled everyone up on to the floor to join in a version of the *syrtáki*, Greece's best-known line dance; the steps are simplified for visitors.

A musician plays a handmade bouzoúki

These dances are usually all accompanied by a fretted lute with four double-strings, the *bouzoúki*, which for many foreigners has become synonymous with all Greek music. In fact, the instrument (which is of Middle Eastern origin) is a comparatively recent import to the island, though the haunting melodies of Manos Hatzidakis and Mikis Theodorakis have made bouzoúki music an intrinsic part of pan-Hellenic folklore.

CHILDREN

It is easy to travel with a family in Greece, and Kefaloniá is a popular destination for those with children. The Greeks are very tolerant – not to say out-and-out indulgent – of children; it is common to see local youngsters late at night in tavernas, learning early on the circadian rhythms of their elders: eating, playing tag and tormenting the cats under the tables, while visitors' children will be accepted

Beach-based activities are a hit with the kids

doing the same. Many of the larger, more expensive hotels and resorts have facilities for children, either full-on kids' clubs or just play areas and dedicated, shallow swimming pools.

Many of the activities already mentioned are suitable for children and the active, outdoor life should appeal greatly to those with an adventurous spirit, with the beach being the obvious focus of activities.

Trekking on horseback around the island is also a possibility (see page 65), though perhaps not advisable for very young children. A visit to the Dhivaráta natural history museum should also go down well with the kids, as will visits to see loggerhead turtles in hatching season – just remember to keep your distance and not to disturb them.

BABY IT'S HOT OUTSIDE

The Mediterranean sun is very strong, especially in the height of the summer holiday season in July and August. Remember that children can burn easily and quickly. Make sure they wear a hat and T-shirt or rash vest and use and top up a high-factor sunscreen at all times, especially when they are in and out of the water. A break in the shade at the hottest part of the day from 12 to 2pm is strongly advisable.

WHAT'S ON

1 January New Year's Day (*Protohroniá*). Feast Day of Ágios Vasilios (St Basil). Before Santa Claus became widespread in Greece, this was the day on which gifts were delivered to children by Äï Vasíli. From Christmas Day to New Year's Day, children sing traditional *kálanda* (songs akin to carols).

6 January Epiphany (*Agía Theofánia* or *Fóta*). In seaside parishes the priest or bishop blesses the waters by throwing a crucifix into the sea, then young men dive in to retrieve it, bestowed with kudos and good luck if they get it.

Easter The great festival of the Greek year. A moveable feast of several stages: **February/March**, *Apókries*, the period before Lent that is Greece's carnival season, celebrated with colourful masquerades and floats; Tsikhnopémpti, 'Grilled Meat Scent Thursday', when psistariés are packed out for a final carnivorous dinner; **Clean Monday**, the first day of Orthodox Lent (*Kathará Dheftéra*), when in good weather everyone goes out for a picnic – the preceding Sunday is the last day the devout consume cheese; **Good Friday**, evening procession of biers (*epitáfii*) of Christ; **Easter Sunday**, at midnight on the Saturday the priest announces *Hristós Anésti* (Christ has risen) and passes the flame of eternal life from the ierón (sanctuary) to the candles of the congregation. This is followed by fireworks, music and dance, and a feast to break the Lenten fast.

25 March Independence Day; also the Annunciation of the Virgin Mary.

1 May May Day. Workers' parades. Wreaths are hung on front doors until St John's Eve (23 June), when they are traditionally burnt on bonfires.

21 May Ionian Islands Union Day (*Énosis ton Eptaníson*) marks the anniversary of the seven islands joining the modern Greek state in 1864.

15 August Dormition of the Virgin Mary (*Kímisis tis Panagías/Theotókou*), celebrated in the village of Markópoulo by a 'snake festival' (6–15 August). .

16 August Feast day of Ágios Gerásimos, patron saint of Kefaloniá (also 20 October).

28 October *Óhi* Day. Celebration of the Greek refusal in 1941 to accept Mussolini's ultimatum, initiating Greece's heroic resistance to Italy's invasion.

25 December Christmas Day; the 26th is also an official holiday.

31 December New Year's Eve (Paramoní tis Protohroniás).

FOOD AND DRINK

Eating Out

At its best, Greek sit-down food is delicious, fresh and well pre-pared; olive oil, tomatoes, onion, garlic, cheese and lemon are all essentials of a simple cuisine. Take an idyllic waterside setting, add charcoal-grilled fish, meat on a spit and a crisp salad, and you have the staples of a typical Greek meal.

Traditionally, a restaurant *(estiatório)* does not have entertain-ment; it is a place for straightforward eating. *Estiatória* (plural) typi-cally provide *magireftá*, oven-cooked or stovetop-casserole dishes that you choose by entering the kitchen and indicating what you want. Meatless *magireftá* is often called *ladhéra* (cooked in oil). In beach resorts, the taverna – with mostly outdoor seating, and thus usually shut from late October to early May – reigns supreme, and ordering by sight is not the rule, except when choosing scaly fish from a chiller case. But neither should you rely on menus – many of these are wishful thinking, issued free to the establishment by a sponsoring drinks company, listing dishes that are never offered. The only reliable bill of fare will be recited by your waiter; check the menu only to verify prices. These usually include a service charge, but diners normally leave 5 to 10 percent extra for the waiter, unless service has been absymal and/or the owner is doing their own waiting. A cover charge (no longer obligatory) includes bread, which varies in quality – darker village bread is excellent. You may decline it; many waiters have begun asking foreigners if they actually want bread, after years of encountering bread left untouched in the basket. Tavernas are more social establishments where customers can spend an entire evening drinking and eating; *psarotavérnes* specialise in fish and seafood. A *psistariá* has rotis-serie and flat grills for cooking meats and poultry.

Islanders have lunch between 2.30 and 4pm, dinner from 9pm onwards, with some establishments taking last orders until 11.15pm. Tavernas aimed at foreigners begin dinner service at around 7pm; you will have your choice of table then, but the atmosphere is definitely better later.

For snacks or even lunch, pop into a bakery for a *tyrópita* (cheese-filled *filo* pastry pie); the *filo*-less version looking like a turnover, called *kouroú*, is less messy and more cheese-filled; if it's stuffed with spinach, it's a *spanakópita*. Meats (usually pork chunks, rarely lamb) grilled on a small skewer are called *souvláki*, while *gýros* are thin slices of pork cut from a vertical rotisserie spit; both are served with garnish, a pinch of chips and *tzatzíki* on pita bread.

> **Some like it hot**
>
> *Magireftá* or *ladherá* dishes are served lukewarm and with lots of olive oil, both considered to promote good digestion. For hot food, ask for it *zestó*; food without oil is *horís ládhi*. However, both such requests will be considered eccentric. Casserole dishes, such as *mousaká*, are cooked for lunchtime and either kept warm all day or just microwave-reheated at night. If you like your food hot or if you are concerned about the hygienic implications of re-heating, order only grilled, fried or marinated dishes in the evening.

MEZÉDHES, OREKTIKÁ AND SALADS

Mezédhes or *orektiká* (appetisers) are small plates of starter food, either cold or hot; carefully selected combinations of *mezédhes* or *orektiká* can constitute a full meal. Shared by the whole table, they are a fun way to eat – you have as little or as much as you want and keep ordering until you have had your fill.

The most common appetisers are *tzatzíki*, a yoghurt dip flavoured with garlic, cucumber and mint; *dolmadhákia*, vine leaves stuffed with rice, onions and herbs, which can be served hot (with egg-lemon sauce) or cold (with dollops of yoghurt); *fáva* (yellow split-pea purée) and *pantzária* (beets), ideally accompanied by a big spoonful of *skordhaliá* (garlic-and-breadcrumb sauce). Mince only appears in *lahanodolmádhes* (stuffed cabbage leaves). Fried *kolokythóanthi* (stuffed squash blossoms) appear in summer and early autumn, often coated in heavy batter; the filling is usually herb-flecked rice. Pale (preferably not pink) *taramosaláta*, fish-roe paste, is served blended with breadcrumbs, olive oil and lemon juice; *aliádha*, similar to the *skordhaliá* garlic purée found throughout Greece, is made with potatoes rather than breadcrumbs, and traditionally served with fried vegetable slices or battered *galéos* (baby dogfish shark). *Melitzanosaláta* is a purée of grilled aubergine, onions, olive oil and garlic, preferably *nistísimo* (without mayonnaise); *tyrokafterí* is a chilli-spicy cheese dip, while *tyropitákia* are small pastry parcels filled with cheese, while *pastourmadhópita* are similar-sized pastry parcels filled with Armenian-style cured beef. *Keftedhákia* are small, fried meatballs bound with breadcrumbs and perhaps egg, flavoured with spices, but *kolokythokeftéedhes* are fried croquettes made with courgettes. *Saganáki* is a hard cheese slice coated in breadcrumbs and then fried, though confusingly the term can also mean a cheese-based red sauce for mussels and shrimp.

Greek salad or *horiátiki saláta* (usually translated as 'village salad') consists of tomato, cucumber, onion, green peppers and olives topped with feta cheese and perhaps a pinch of dried *throúmbi* (summer savory). During cooler spring months, you may be offered a salad of finely shredded lettuce (*maroúli*) with spring onions and dill. *Ambelofásola*, steamed or boiled green/runner beans, available from late June into September, are considered a salad in Greece, as are *kolokythákia* (courgettes), boiled whole and served drowned in

Restaurant in Assos

olive oil, and *hórta* (boiled wild chicory greens or – more typically in midsummer – cultivated amaranth leaves), served lukewarm or at room temperature, again with oil and vinegar or lemon. Come autumn, cabbage/carrot salad (*lahanokaróto*) appears, often with too much cabbage and not enough grated carrot.

All salads should arrive at the table dressed with olive oil and vinegar. If you require more oil, sealed, mini bottles of oil can be provided (for which there is an additional charge by law, although it is not always imposed). Cruets of olive oil and wine vinegar may still be found with other condiments on the table, attached to the napkin rack.

MAIN COURSES: MEATS AND CASSEROLES

Common oven dishes include *mousaká* (minced meat, aubergine and potato slices with béchamel sauce and a cheese topping), brought to Greece by refugees from Asia Minor, but ultimately

Classic Greek Souvláki

originating in the Arab world; and *pastítsio* (macaroni and mincemeat pie topped with béchamel sauce. *Kléftiko* is Cypriot-style lamb, slowly baked until it is very tender, while *stifádho* is beef or rabbit (*kounéli*) braised with pearl onions. You may also come across *gídha vrastí* (boiled goats' meat, served in a broth with potatoes). *Briám* or *tourlou* (a ratatouille of potatoes, tomatoes and courgettes) and *fasolákia ladherá* (green beans stewed with tomato, herbs and oil) are two other popular casserole dishes, while *fasoládha* (white bean soup) is a winter favourite. Springtime treats include fresh *angináres* (artichokes), which may be found at other times of the year as defrosted hearts in *angináres ala políta* (stewed in a white broth with potatoes and carrots), and *koukiá* (fresh broad beans, May only; otherwise rehydrated). *Bámies* (okra) are also particularly good, most commonly served in mid-summer in a soup-like sauce known as *yahní*. Another more substantial hot meatless dish are *gemistés,* tomatoes or peppers stuffed with herb-flavoured rice (though meat stock may be used); alternatively, *melitzánes imám* (aubergine richly prepared with tomato, onions and oil) is reliably vegetarian, as are *gígandes* (pale, hard-to-digest haricot beans served in a *yahní* sauce).

Sit-down barbecued dishes include whole chickens, *kondosoúvli* (rotisserie-grilled pork) and *gouronópolo* (spit-roasted suckling piglet); the latter is usually only available at weekends when there is sufficient clientele to justify lighting the enormous bank of coals required to cook it. If you want a basic pork cutlet, ask for a *brizóla*; a veal chop is a *spalobrizóla*; lamb or goat chops, however, are *païd-hákia*. *Souvláki* is also served as a main sit-down course in tavernas and psistariés, as are *pantsétes*, which resemble American spare ribs. *Biftékia*, grilled or baked 'hamburgers', sometimes stuffed with rich cheese for extra artery-clogging properties, are ubiquitous. *Giouvétsi* is beef or lamb, cooked in a pot with orzo pasta and tomato. *Soutzoukákia* are rolls of minced meat cooked in tomato sauce. *Giouvarlákia* are rolls of minced meat covered in egg-and-lemon sauce *(avgolémono)* or swimming in a thinner, almost clear broth. More unusual foods you may encounter include *kokorétsi* (spit-grilled lamb's offal wrapped in intestines), or sheep/pork testicles, known as 'unmentionables' *(amelétita)*. *Pátsas* is tripe, served up in a spicy soup, much vaunted as a hangover cure. If you are on Kefaloniá at Easter weekend, you may break the Lenten fast with the islanders just after Saturday midnight with tasty *magirítsa*, a soup made from finely chopped lamb's offal and dill. Whole spit-roasted lamb (or goat) is the main feature of Easter Sunday midday outings.

Desserts are not usually on the menu except in the most touristy eateries – think *panna cotta* or *tiramisu* – but often offered on the house with the bill as a *kérazma* (sweet treat). These include yoghurt with honey, often with walnut pieces; *simigdhalísios halvás*, made with semolina; *kormós*, a chunk of chocolate loaf; and *glyká tou koutaliou*, 'spoon' sweets, candied fruit, usually grapes, bergamot or cherries. Sometimes you will encounter *galaktoboúreko*, filo pastry filled with custard and topped by syrup; *baklavás*, made of crushed nuts in filo pastry, soaked in syrup; *karydhópita*, walnut cake, or *ravaní*, sponge cake, either of these doused in varying amounts of syrup. During mid-summer, the *kérazma* may only be a plate of the most abundant seasonal fruit: grapes, figs, chunks of Persian melon or watermelon.

A *zaharoplastío* (sticky-cake shop) offers decadent oriental sweets: *baklavás* or *galaktoboúreko*, as described above; or *kataïfi*, 'shredded wheat' filled with chopped almonds and honey. Quality ice-cream, including proper gelato, has arrived in Greece with a vengeance. Anywhere with many Italian tourists (including Kefaloniá) should support at least one passably genuine *gelateria*, possibly even Italian-owned and staffed.

SEAFOOD AND FISH

Fish sizes vary from the tiny picarel *(marídhes)* and summertime sardines *(sardhéles)* or sand smelt *(atherína)*, to the larger dentex *(synagrídha)*, swordfish *(xifías)* or dusky grouper *(rofós)*. In between are red mullet *(barboúni)* or the smaller, less expensive, related goatfish *(koutsomoúra)* and several breams *(tsipoúra, fangrí, sargós* and *melanoúri)*. *Skorpína* (grilled or baked scorpion fish is much esteemed, as is fresh small hake *(bakalarákia)*. Larger fish is usually grilled and smaller fish fried, though sardines are ideally grilled, then served *petáli* (butterflied) and deboned. Staff can sometimes be reluctant to agree to grilling sardines, claiming that the too-small specimen will far apart, but it is worth insisting. If coals are not lit, there should be

PSAROTAVÉRNES

These can be very expensive but will have some fresh fish unless winds have kept the boats in harbour, or it's the heart of closed season (June–Sept) when mega-trawlers and other indiscriminate fishing methods cannot be used. A good rule of thumb to guarantee fresh, not defrosted, fare is to only order seasonal fish. All scaly fish is sold by weight (before it is cleaned) and you might want to keep an eye on the scales; also look out for fish marked *katapsygméno* (frozen), sometimes just with an asterix, 'kat' or 'k' on menus.

a gas range for grilling. The most common big species, served with fresh lemon and *ladholémono* (a cruet of olive oil with lemon juice), include red mullet and swordfish. Grilled octopus *(htapódi)* and cuttlefish *(soupiá)* are delicious, and deep-fried squid *(kalamarákia)*, though often defrosted, are often available. *Gónos* (hatchlings) may refer to baby whole squid, or to any small fish. You may also (except from Sept–Dec) find spiny lobster *(astakós)*,

Kefalonián thyme honey

often flaked and cooked with spaghetti *(astakomakaronádha)* but occasionally grilled on the half-shell. Another, somewhat rarer Aegean crustacean is the slipper lobster *(kolokhtýpes)*.

LOCAL DISHES

There are a few Kefalonián specialities, some of which bear testimony to their history of invasion and occupation. There is much influence from Italy (specifically Venice) throughout the Ionian islands, for example in dishes such as *sofríto*, lightly fried or stewed veal with garlic and vinegar; *bourdhéto*, white-fleshed fish stewed with tomatoes, hot red peppers, onions, garlic and olive oil; *biánko*, as its name implies, is a 'white', tomato-less fish stew with lots of garlic, potatoes, onions, lemon, oil, black pepper and white wine. *Pastitsádha* is cockerel in sauce served with thick, round noodles.

Kefaloniá has its own *kreatópita*, a pie consisting of meat and rice flavoured with cinnamon and topped with a thick pastry. This is widely available, while rather more unusual is the octopus pie traditionally eaten during Lent. Also remarkable is *kofisópita*, made from salted fish.

A Kefalonián quirk is *aliádha*, essentially the same as the *skordhaliá* garlic purée found elsewhere in Greece, but made with potatoes rather than breadcrumbs.

There are 14 local dairies, producing primarily cheeses from blended sheep and goat milk, including a so-called *varelísio* (barrelled) *féta*, plus hard, sharper *graviéra* and *kefalograviéra*. The three biggest cheese-makers, their products widely available on the island, include *Galiatsatos*, *Georgetos* and *Pantzatos*. All dairies also produce yoghurt, obviously not a very portable souvenir but well worth tucking into while on the island.

By the roadside you may see thyme honey (*thymarísio méli*) sold in large jars. If possible, sample from the same batch before buying. Getting stuck with a jar of bogus thyme honey is a risk; the strong, aromatic odour of the real deal, wafting from the container, is unmistakeable. Spathis is one widely promoted honey brand. But this is not the only sweet speciality. *Amygdhalópita* (almond pie), traditionally baked in a round tin, is a Kefalonián favourite, as is *kydhonópasto*, a quince paste similar to Spanish *membrillo* but here studded with almond pieces.

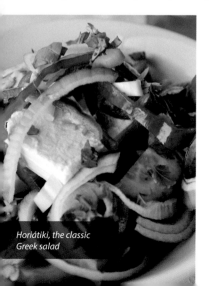

Horiátiki, the classic Greek salad

WHAT TO DRINK

In the summer you will need to drink a lot of water, but do try to steer clear of bottled 'spring' water, as Greece's mountain of plastic bottles is growing ever higher. Tap water is perfectly safe on Kefaloniá, though it is hard. If you carry your own water bottle, cafés and restaurants you visit will be happy to fill it for you, with cooled tap water. Better still, find one of the islands' well-regarded springs, from which locals often take their own drinking water.

Greece has delicious bottled fizzy lemonade (lemonádha), which, unlike some 'lemon drinks', does actually contain lemon juice; the best brands are Epsa and Loux. Numerous beer labels are produced in Greece, including by local microbreweries. Foreign brands made under licence include Amstel, Kaiser and Fischer; the best two mainstream Greek labels are Fix and Mamos, but other good ones include Nymfi, Alfa, Mythos and Vergina (especially its red, high-alcohol lager). Kefalonia has its very own microbrewery (www.Kefaloniánbeer.com), producing a premium lager (5 percent) and a red ale (5.8 percent).

Another drink worth looking out for is soumádha, a thick syrup made from almonds, often wild. Diluted with chilled water, there is nothing more refreshing on a hot summer's day. Sealed 700ml bottles of it are sold as souvenirs.

Greece has been making wine for millennia and, although in the past some of its wines have been particularly esteemed, few are now well known outside the country owing to small annual production. Many wineries struggle to exceed 10,000 bottles a year.

Kefaloniá is a significant wine-producing island and is particularly noted for whites made from the Robóla grape, which has attracted a PDO appellation. The vines grow well in the dry, stony soils common on the island, and it is possible to visit a number of the best wineries (see pages 39 and 42). Many have branched out in recent decades to producing reds and rosés.

Exotic Cuisine

If you tire of local fare, you can usually find everything from international gourmet cuisine to ethnic fare, from Chinese stir-fry to crêpes. Don't turn your nose up at Italian food in particular – the Greeks love pizza and pasta dishes, while the numerous Italian visitors demand high standards.

Failing local wines, mainland labels to watch for in tavernas and shops include three top-drawer, medium-priced reds (Ktima Papaïoannou, Tsantali Rapsani and almost anything from Nemea). For a premium mainland white, try the Spyropoulos, Tselepos and Skoura vintners from the Peloponnese, and the two Lazaridhi wineries from Dhráma, Macedonia. Rosé wine from Amýndeo and surroundings, in western Macedonia, is also reliably quaffable.

Barrelled/bulk wines (*hýma*), usually but not always local, can be surprisingly good, or almost undrinkable; if you're unsure, ask to sample it before committing to a large measure. Resinated wine (*retsína*) can also be good, particularly when served very cold with oily food.

Spirits (Potá)

Anise-flavoured *oúzo* is taken as an aperitif with ice and water; a compound in the anise flavouring makes the mix turn harmlessly cloudy. The most popular brands (like Mini, Varvagianni and Plomari) come from Lésvos Island, though on Kefaloniá you may well find Pilavas which is imported from Pátra on the mainland. At tavernas, *oúzos* come in sealed 200ml *karafákia* (mini bottles meant for two diners). *Tsípouro* is a mainland variant of this grape-mash distillate, best without anise (*horís glykániso*), similar to Italian *grappa*. The best, most common mass-market label is Apostolaki from Thessaly; you may also be offered *hýma tsípouro* in measures of up to 500ml.

All such drinks are typically served with a small ice bucket; place cubes in your glass, then pour the *oúzo* or *tsípouro* on top, adding water as needed (in summer the ice quickly melts, so don't over-dilute it or you will end up with something akin to soda pop).

Non-alcoholic drinks

Hot coffee (*kafés*) comes as *ellínikós* (generic Middle Eastern or Turkish style, renamed 'Greek' in patriotic pique after the various Cyprus crises), freshly brewed in small copper pots (*bríkia*) and served in small cups. It will probably arrive *glykós* (sweet) unless you order *métrios* (medium) or *skétos* (without sugar); extra sweet is *varýglykos*. These are always accompanied by a glass of chilled water. Don't drink to the bottom as that's where the grounds settle; a *kafetzoú* (a Greek grandmother skilled in this art) can tell your fortune from the patterns left in this sediment.

Instant coffee is generically known as *nes* or *néskafe*, irrespective of brand; it's pretty unpalatable and headache-inducing, an extra-strength formula concocted for Mediterranean tastes. Since the millennium there has been a backlash against it, so in large resorts and Argostóli you can easily find proper brewed coffee (*gallikós* or *fíltros*), as well as a competently executed cappuccino and espresso. *Fredduccino* – cold cappuccino – is also seasonally popular. Any milky coffee (though never with *ellinikós*) is *me gála*.

Frappés, cold instant coffee whipped up in a blender with sugar, ice chips and milk, is quite an established drink. This looks a bit like a small Guinness and tastes like a coffee milkshake, but it's surprisingly refreshing in hot weather.

Soft drinks come in all the international varieties, while Greek-bottled juices are most likely out of cardboard cartons. Bottled (*enfialoméno*) still mineral water is typically from Crete or the Greek mainland mountains. Souroti, Loux and Epsa are the most common domestic sparkling brands. Soda water is usually Tuborg brand.

TO HELP YOU ORDER…AND PAY

Is there a table available, please? **Ypárhi éna diathésimo trapézi, parakaló?**

Could we reserve a table for tonight? **Boroúme na klísoume éna trapézi yia apópse?**

May we order, please? **Na parangiloúme, parakaló?**

I'd like a/some… **Tha íthela éna (m), mía (f)/meriká(n)…**

I'm a vegetarian **Íme hortofágos/hortogági**

I'm a vegan **Móno tró nistísima piáta; Íme végan**

I have an allergy to… **Ého allergía se…**

Cheers! (as a toast) **Yiámas!**

A litre/a half litre (of *hýma* wine or *tsípouro*) **Éna kiló/misó kilo**

Enjoy the rest of your meal (literally, 'Good continuation') **Kalí synnéhia**

The bill, please. **To logariazmó, parakaló.**

BASIC CONDIMENTS, FOODS, UTENSILS

oil **ládhi**	napkins **hartopetsétes**
glass **potíri**	eggs **avgá**
plate **piáto**	yoghurt **yiaoúrti**
cutlery **maheropírouna**	onions **kremmýdhia**
bread (wholemeal) **psomí (olikís aléseos)**	pasta **(noodles) makarónia**
	honey **méli**
butter **voútyro**	black pepper **mávro pipéri**
sugar (brown) **záhari (kastaní)**	rice **rýzi**
	lemon **lemóni**
salt **aláti**	butter **voútyro**
black pepper mávro **pipéri**	vinegar **xýdi**

READING THE MENU (KATÁLOGOS)

boiled **vrastó**	fried **tiganitó**

baked **sto foúrno**
roasted **psitó**
spit-roasted **soúvlas**
grilled **sta kárvouna**

MEZÉDHES, OREKTIKÁ

marinated small anchovies
    antzoúgies
fried large anchovies **gávros**
stuffed squash blossoms
    kolokythóanthi
stuffed vine-leaves
    dolmádhes
olives **eliés**
cheese **tyrí**
beets **pantzária**
split yellow peas **fáva**
fried courgette croquettes
    kolokythokeftédhes
chickpea fritters (like falafel)
    revythokeftédhes
fried small courgettes
    kolokythákia tiganitá
fried aubergine slices
    melitzánes tiganités
fried cheese **saganáki**
mushroom pie **manitarópita**
onion pie **kremmydhópita**
spinach filo pie **spanakópita**
grey mullet- or cod-roe dip
    taramosaláta
cheese pies **tyropitákia**
yoghurt dip with garlic and
    cucumber **tzatziki**

MEAT (KRÉAS)

sausages **loukánika**
small fried meatballs
    keftedhákia
beef **vodhinó kréas**
veal **moskhári**
pork **hirinó**
chicken **kotópoulo**
lamb **arní**
kid goat katsíki, katsikáki
rabbit **kounéli**
hot pot with meat and orzo
    giouvétsi
formed mince 'hamburger'
    biftéki
pork chop **brizóla**
veal chop **spalobrizóla**
meatballs baked in red sauce
    soutzoukákia

garlic-flavoured **skórdháto**
red sauce for vegetables
    yahní

FISH (PSÁRI) AND SEAFOOD (THALASSINÁ)

fresh **frésko**

frozen **katapsygméno**

brine-cured **pastó(s)**

cured bonito slices **lakérdha**

small shrimp (often
in *saganáki* sauce)
garidhákia

bigger grilling shrimp
garídhes

octopus **okhtapódhi,
khtapódhi**

red mullet **barboúni**

goatfish (small red mullet)
koutsomoúra

swordfish **xifías**

fresh small hake **bakalarákia**

picarel **marídhes**

sand-smelt, silverside
atherína

baby squid **kalamarákia,
gónos**

mussels **mýdhia**

sardines **sardhéles**

cuttlefish **soupiá**

VEGETABLES

salad **saláta**

'Greek' salad **horiátiki saláta**

lettuce **maroúli**

green onion **frésko
kremmýdhi**

dill **ánitho**

cabbage-carrot salad
láhano-karóto

tomatoes **domátes**

olives **eliés**

boiled greens **hórta**

runner/string beans
ambelofásola

artichokes (stewed hearts)
angináres (ala políta)

peas **arakádhes**

baked stuffed tomatoes
domátes yemistés

baked stuffed bell peppers
piperiés yemistés

cheese-stuffed fried
long peppers **piperies
yemistés me tyrí**

aubergine **melitzána**

chickpeas, stewed **revýthia**

potatoes, fried/roasted
**patátes tiganités/sto
foúrno**

pale haricot beans **fasólia
yígandes**

courgettes (boiled)
kolokythákia

FRUITS

apple **mílo**

orange **portokáli**

grapes **stafýlia**

figs **sýka**

watermelon **karpoúzi**

apricots **verýkoka**

Persian melon **pepóni**

WHERE TO EAT

The following prices reflect the average cost of a two-course meal (per person) plus a half litre of *hýma* (barrelled house wine). At all restaurants an automatic tax of 13 percent (VAT) is always included in the menu-listed prices of food and non-alcoholic drinks; all booze, whether beer, wine or stronger spirits, is taxed at 24 percent. If service has been good, it is customary to leave an additional five to 10 percent for the waiter, especially if they are obviously an employee and not the owner. Most town restaurants operate year round but those in the resorts and villages only from May to October, unless otherwise stated.

€€€€	**over 45 euros**
€€€	**35–45 euros**
€€	**22–35 euros**
€	**below 22 euros**

KEFALONIÁ

Argostóli

There are a few places on or just off Platía Valliánou that are good for breakfast, a snack or for simply sitting with a drink.

Arhontiko €€ *Rizospastón 5, tel: 26710 27213*. This compact, friendly taverna working out of a stone building has seating on a small outside patio, where you tuck into such hearty platters as *exohikó* (baked lamb), *strapatsádha* (egg-and-vegetable hotpot) or *biftéki* in Roquefort sauce. *Mezédhes* and wine are excellent too.

Captain's Table €€€ *Andóni Trítsi 143 near ferry dock;* https://captainstable-restaurant.com. Occupying sleek modern premises on the seafront (with outdoor seating on wooden decking), this serves hearty but creatively presented dishes such as butterflied grilled scaly fish or grilled squid, plus meaty specials like lamb shank. Live *kandádes* on Saturday, more frequently in season. Also does breakfast/brunch, a variety of own-made desserts, and cocktails.

Casa Grec €€ *Stavrou Metaxa 12, tel: 26710 24091*. Mouth-watering, value-for-money Mediterranean fare served in a charming ambiance, though not the best spot in town for seafood. Bacon-and-cheese-stuffed Portobello mushrooms and smoked pork chop are two standout dishes. Evenings only until 2am.

Kyani Akti €€€ *Ioánnou Metaxá 1, far north end of the quay;* https://kyani-akti.business.site. A superb *psarotavérna* built out over the sea. Their speciality is, unsurprisingly, fresh fish and seafood, and they often have unusual recipes to try, such as ravioli stuffed with stone crab, halloúmi cheese and *astakós*. But there is also a range of vegetarian (even vegan) dishes like cauliflower steak, grilled broccoli with feta and roasted almonds, and authentic meat recipes such as slow-roasted goat, plus excellent house wine.

Portside Taverna €€ *Ioánni Metaxá 58, tel: 26710 24130*. The friendly Portside Taverna (unsurprisingly overlooking the port) has excellent seafood dishes such as marinated tuna or locally caught swordfish, surprisingly good house wine and agreeable service.

Tzivras € *V. Vandhórou 1, tel: 27610 24259 or 697 473 5749*. Classic old-fashioned *estiiatório*, founded in 1933. Only open until late afternoon, but great for oven-baked casserole dishes like *mousaká*, *kreatópita*, *gemistés* and *briám*.

Lixoúri and the south

Agrapidhos € *Póros, just uphill from the port, tel: 26710 72480*. Good all-rounder taverna with the usual range of appetizers and mains including *mousaká*, and decent house rosé wine. Open Apr–Oct.

Akrogiali € *Lixoúri quay (Andréa Laskaratou 21), towards south end, tel: 26710 92613*. An enduring, budget-priced institution, with considerable local clientele. Wholesome and tasty food with an emphais on oven-casserole food (including *giouvétsi* and *kreatópita*), but also fish and grills in the evening, plus excellent house wine.

Blue Sea €€€ *Káto Katélios, tel: 26710 81122*. The fish here is famously fresh, sourced from the little anchorage adjacent, and superbly cooked. Bills might just fall into the €€ category if you order carefully and stick to *hýma* wine. Open May–Oct.

Botsolos € *On the road between Valsamáta and Agíou Gerasímou, tel: 26710 86156.* Psistariá with outdoor seating under trees; it offers up a good selection of dishes such as liver and lamb chops, preceded by typical Greek salads and *mezédhes*. The best lunch stop before or after performing your devotions at the monastery.

Fotis Family € *Póros, tel: 26740 72972.* Set in a delightful position, built into the headland at the end of the town beach, with great views across the straits to Itháki. The menu emphasises a variety of fresh fish, but there are also meat platters, tasty *mezédhes* and salads. A good option while waiting for a ferry.

Karnagio €€ *Miaoúli (seafront) 46, Sámi, tel: 6939 582 041.* With a decent selection of vegetable and meat dishes, including the local specialty meat pie, this is the best of the central quay port-side tavernas. It's also good for its fresh off teh boat seafood, including tuna steak and (occasionally) grouper. Apr–Oct.

Lorraine's Magic Hill €€ *Lourdháta, tel: 26710 31605,* https://lorrainesrestaurant.gr. Perched on a hillside just above the beach, this gem run by the very friendly American lady it is named after, dishes up huge portions of traditional fare such as liver, roast goat and *giouvétsi* (meat cooked in a clay pot with *kritharáki* (orzo), though not much seafood. Great place for a cocktail too. May–Oct daily 6–11pm.

Ta Pitharia €€ *Skála,* https://tavernatapitharia.gr/en/tavern-skala-kefalonia. The best taverna in the village provides a range of *mezédhes*, oven dishes and roasts like *kondosoúvli* (spit-roasted pork), or you can opt for a massive steak. May–Oct daily.

Xouras € *Petaní beach, Lixoúri peninsula, tel: 26710 97458.* Right behind the middle of one of the island's best beaches and run by welcoming Greek-American Dina, this is a great spot for sunset dining. Grills and fish are the specialities, alongside a selection of excellent salads and some *magireftá* (casserole dishes).

The north

Amalia € *Around the headland from Agía Evfimía harbour to the northeast, tel: 26740 61088*. Located around the headland past the harbour, this is the place for moderately priced island cuisine such as small fried fish and local sausage. Open May–Oct.

Makis € *Vasilikiádhes, tel: 26740 51556*. You can enjoy a wonderful, inexpensive and extremely authentic meal in the large courtyard of this inland village *psistariá*. Expect succulent grilled lamb chops, as well as fine *mezédhes* such as *kolokythokeftedes* (cheese-laced courgette patties). Also does good desserts.

Nefeli-Anait €€ *Ássos, tel: 26740 51251*, www.nefeli-anait.com. One of four establishments overlooking the very attractive harbour, this all-rounder taverna offers the usual range of salads and a few grilled and oven dishes, as well as fresh seafood. There is good barrelled wine and a selection of other drinks.

Odysseas € *Agía Ierousalím, tel: 26740 41133*. A true hidden gem. You are assured a warm welcome and relaxed dining experience from the owner, while his mother churns out the grub. All their ingredients are organic or free range and you can sample delights such as olive bread, slow-cooked lamb and ultra-fresh salads, all washed down with their fine house wine. They also have homemade honey, jam and other produce for sale. Open Apr–Oct.

Platanos € *Ássos, tel: 26740 51381*. Set just back from the seafront under the huge namesake plane tree, this is good for grilled meat such as suckling pig and fish, as well as casserole dishes. There's also a wide selection of salads and starters, plus aromatic local wine. Open Apr–Oct.

Spyros € *Agía Evfimía, tel: 26740 61739*. A wide range of specials such as lamb *kléftiko*, saffron chicken with rice, and beef ragout under yoghurt sauce can be enjoyed at this friendly taverna halfway along the waterfront. Open May–Sept.

Tassia €€€ *Apolitos wharf, Fiskárdho, tel: 26740 41205*, https://www.tassia.gr. A nice harbourfront spot with lovely views of Itháki. This was the first (1972) restaurant established in Fiskárdho. Acclaimed owner-chef Tassia Dendrinou offers traditional Kefalonián dishes cooked creatively. Seafood is a must here, especially the octopus in wine, but can get pricey. Extensive wine list. Dinner only, from 4pm.

To Foki € *at the head of Fóki Bay, tel: 697 819 7524*. This very pleasant and friendly taverna, situated just opposite the beach, serves simple but tasty food – *fáva*, *souvláki* and salads – and lovely *milópita* (apple pie). Reasonably priced, quaffable *hýma* wine. Much better value than anything to be found in Fiskárdho just down the road. Do take mosquito repellent for the evenings.

Vasso's €€€ *southeast end of main quay, Fiskárdho, tel: 26740 41276* http://vassosrestaurant.com. *Magireftá* with a difference: olive tapenade for your bread, plus creative desserts. Reasonably priced, for Fiskárdho at least, if you stay away from lobster and other more expensive fish and seafood species.

Itháki

Avra €€ *Kióni tel: 26740 31453*. Harbourside taverna that offers the usual selection of salads, some dips and a good choice of mainly grilled meat, plus fish courses to suit all budgets. May–Sept daily.

Odysseus € *Fríkes, tel: 26740 31733*. Popular restaurant at mid-seafront specializing in succulent home-style cuisine: it also serves plenty of lighter snacks, sweets and beverages. Open May–Oct.

O Tseligas (aka Mousáki) €€ *Stavrós, tel: 26740 31596*. Not easy to miss thanks to its bright yellow building and awnings, this welcoming place dishes up great *mezédhes* plus *kondosoúvli* and *kokorétsi*, but is best known for *tserépa* (chicken or lamb baked with potatoes and peppers). May to early Oct.

To Kohili € *Vathý, tel: 26740 33565*. By far the best of the half-dozen harbourside tavernas, with seating on the quay or in the leafy garden round the corner. They serve a good range of *mezédhes*, as well as tasty meat dishes such as lamb *kléftiko*, *giouvétsi* and *soutzoukákia*, plus grills and pasta.

Trehantiri € *Vathý, tel: 26740 33444*. Tucked a block back from the seafront on Dhoríou, this family-run taverna does good home-cooking displayed in trays, think fish soup, onion pie, slow-cooked pork and goat. Open Apr–Oct.

TRAVEL ESSENTIALS

PRACTICAL INFORMATION

A

ACCOMMODATION

Hotels. Many hotels are heavily booked with package tours in summer, especially between early July and early September, when advance reservations are strongly recommended. Recourse to the usual third-party booking websites can be successful; in slow years package operators have online specials, or try the locally based website of villa owners, www.kefalonia-villas.com. However, be aware that by booking though Greek websites, you forego any of the legal/financial protections afforded by using a UK-based and -bonded ABTA member.

Hotels, always with en-suite bathrooms, are rated from 2-star to 5-star, based more on their common areas and amenities than the actual rooms. Prices can vary widely within each category, while ultra-luxury (5-star) establishments are not price controlled. Thus, a 3-star hotel room may be just as comfortable as a 5-star room, but common areas will not include a conference room, hairdresser, gym, spa or multiple restaurants. All hotels of 3-star rating and above are reasonably furnished, and should provide breakfast, usually included in the rate.

Villas and apartments. There are many villas, apartments and studios (the latter two terms interchangeable) in Kefaloniá available to rent. Accommodation ranges from simple rooms to lavishly appointed summer homes complete with a swimming pool.

In the UK, companies offering top-of-the-range secluded luxury villas on Kefaloniá include:

Greek Islands Club/The Villa Collection, www.gicthevillacollection.com/kefalonia/intro

---

I'd like a single/double room/family apartment **Tha íthela éna monóklino/díklino domátio/ikoyeniakó dhiamérizma**
What's the rate per night? **Póso stihízi yia káthe vrádhi?**

CV Villas, www.cvvillas.com/destinations/greece/kefalonia
James Villa Holidays, tel: 0800 074 0122, www.jamesvillas.co.uk
Simpon Travel, tel: 020 8392 5858, www.simpsontravel.com

AIRPORTS

Kefaloniá's Yanna Pollatou Airport is located 7km (just over 4 miles) southeast of Argostóli: it was thoroughly overhauled by German operator Fraport between 2017 and 2019. If you have booked your holiday through a UK tour operator you will be met at the airport and whisked off in a coach to your villa or resort, otherwise you will have to take one of up to six buses into town (only during tourist season; see https://ktelkefalonias.gr/en/routes/local-routes), or a taxi to wherever you are staying (consult https://kefaloniataxis.com for an idea of what you will pay). Kefaloniá is connected domestically by air to Athens (four–five flights daily, 1hr); Corfu (summer three flights weekly, 2hrs); Zákynthos (summer three flights weekly, 25 mins); Préveza (summer three flights weekly, 30 mins). For a comprehensive table of flight arrivals and departures, consult www.efl-airport.gr/en/flight-list

B

BICYCLE AND MOTORCYCLE HIRE

You can hire motorcycles and quad bikes in all the tourist centres. However, many package operators warn clients against motorised cycles and scooters for the quite legitimate fear of an accident (and to drum up business for their organised excursions). It is vital that you check that motorbike hire does not invalidate your holiday insurance. Scooter hire is affordable (you should be quoted a rate per day, or sometimes per week, including third-party insurance and CDW collision-damage waiver). To hire a motorbike with an engine of 50–90cc displacement you must be at least 18 years old and hold a driving license authorised for Class AM (look on the back of a UK one). US licenses must include Class M, and be accompanied by an International Driving Permit, issued by AAA offices in the US or the CAA in Canada. Rental agencies have become quite strict on this point – zealous police are fining both them and riders up to €1,000 for contraventions. If you don't possess the appropriate licence(s), which must be carried with you as you drive, agencies will push you to hire a quad bike; however these are notoriously unstable, and crash helmets will be pointedly provided. It is in fact illegal to ride two-wheeled scooters without a crash helmet – the fines issued at checkpoints are similarly draconian, payable at a major post office.

It is inadvisable to ride a motorbike in shorts or a swimsuit, since burns or scrapes resulting from even a slight accident could be appalling; clinics and hospital casualty wards are wearily familiar with treating 'road rash'. Test brakes, lights and tyres before hiring, and drive with care. Even on 'good' roads there are potholes or treacherous stretches of loose gravel.

BUDGETING FOR YOUR TRIP

Kefaloniá is not the cheapest of the Greek islands, and these days it is probably as costly as most other Mediterranean destinations. In high season, the rate for a 4-star hotel is around €200 minimum per night for a double room. Booking an airfare/accommodation package will yield substantial savings. Otherwise, independent travellers can find return flights from the UK for around £100–200 on scheduled airlines like BA or easyJet, decent places to stay from around €60–80 per night for a double room, with big discounts available outside of peak summer season.

Eating out is considerably cheaper if you stick to *magireftá*, simple grills and *mezédhes* in places also frequented by locals: generally a three-course meal plus drinks in a decent restaurant or taverna will cost around €15–25 per person, assuming two or more adult diners. Public transport and museum fees are inexpensive.

C

CAR HIRE

Unless visiting the island with the intention of walking or cycling, you might consider hiring a car on Kefaloniá, where the bus service is very patchy. As with anywhere in Greece, car hire is not particularly cheap, but it is certainly less expensive than touring by taxi. Car hire starts from about €30 per day in low season (with a €500–800 insurance excess for damage). For a decent family-sized car in high season, you should budget at least €300 per week; all have air conditioning these days.

Better third-party consolidator websites include www.auto-europe.co.uk, www.carrentals.co.uk and www.rentalcargroup.com. Post-Brexit, UK licences are honoured for now, but it's wise to secure an IDP from any major UK post office branch before departure; bring your UK licence (minimum age 18) and one passport-sized photo. On payment of a small fee (currently £5.50), it should be issued on the spot.

You'll find car-hire firms across Kefaloniá, at least in tourist resorts. To be on the safe side, reserve a car well ahead of time, especially for the high season – a week before won't do. Local firms generally charge slightly less than inter-national agencies and provide equally good cars and service; Auto Kefalonia is one such company https://autokefalonia.com. International chains that oper-ate here, often through affiliates but bookable through their websites, include Avis, Budget, Europcar, Hertz, National, Sixt and Thrifty.

Many brochure rates seem attractive because they do not include personal insurance, collision damage waiver (CDW) or VAT at 24 percent. Most agencies have a waiver excess of between €400 and €750 – the amount (pre-blocked on your credit card) you're responsible for if your vehicle gets smashed or stolen, even with CDW coverage. It is strongly suggested you purchase extra cover (often called Super CDW or Liability Waiver Surcharge) to reduce this risk to zero; UK or North American residents can buy good-value annual policies from enti-ties like Insurance4CarHire (www.insurance4carhire.com) or iCar Hire Insurance (www.icarhireinsurance.com). Policies sold on the spot are invariably rip-offs.

When you pick up the car, video the walk round with the agent so you don't get charged for anyone else's scratches and dings.

You will almost always need a credit card for the deposit (though you may pay the actual rental charge with a debit card) and a full national licence (held for at least one year) from your country of residence. If you are from a non-EU country, it is also mandatory to have an International Driving Permit (IDP) – another little-known law which is increasingly enforced. Depending on the model and the hire company, the minimum age for hiring a car varies from 21 to 25. Third-party liability insurance (CDW) is usually included in the stated rate, but with an excess amount that can be up to €800, so it is always worth paying a little more for comprehensive coverage, particularly a policy that insures you for a crash with a third party.

What's the hire charge for a full day/for a full week? **Póso kostízi giá mía méra/gia mia evdhomádha?**

I'd like to hire a car (tomorrow) **Tha íthela na nikiáso éna aftokínito (ávrio)**

CLIMATE

July and August are the sunniest, hottest and busiest tourist months. You may prefer to visit between mid-May and late June or from early September to mid-October. It can rain at any time of year, though much less likely in July and Aug. The Ionians are the greenest of all the Greek island chains, because during winter it rains very hard. November and December are the wettest

	J	F	M	A	M	J	J	A	S	O	N	D
Air temperatures												
°C	9	10	12	15	18	23	26	26	22	19	14	13
°F	48	50	54	59	64	74	79	79	72	66	59	55
Sea temperatures												
°C	16	15	15	16	19	23	25	26	25	23	20	17
°F	61	59	59	61	66	73	77	79	75	73	68	63
Sunshine hours												
	6	7	8	10	12	13	14	13	10	8	7	6

months and January the coldest, but even during mid-winter the climate is moderate, with hard freezes very very rare except on the mountaintops. Spring, when the island bursts with wild flowers, is the best time for walking or cycling through the countryside.

The chart opposite shows each month's average air and sea temperature in Celsius and Fahrenheit, and the average number of hours of sunshine per day.

CLOTHING

Clothing is invariably casual on the islands. However, the Greeks do dress up when going out in the evening and visitors who make a bit of an effort will be smiled upon – conversely, beach garb, except at lunchtime by the sea, is frowned on. With regard to comfort, choose lightweight cotton clothing in spring and summer, and a warm jacket, sweater and rainwear in autumn and winter – waterproof gear is also useful for seagoing excursions. Since it rains from time to time, a protective coat or umbrella outside of July and August might be a good idea. Plastic shoes or 'trekking' sandals are extremely useful for (hot) stony beaches; these are available to purchase from beach-side tourist shops.

CRIME AND SAFETY (SEE ALSO EMERGENCIES)

The Kefaloniáns are, like the vast majority of Greek people, scrupulously honest. However, unfortunately, thefts occur, so it's sensible to leave valuables in the hotel safe. Look after your passport but at the same time be aware that you're required to have official ID on your person at all times in Greece; a photocopy should suffice for beach outings.

Possession of drugs is a very serious matter in Greece, carrying a stiff mandatory sentence and potentially long spells being held on remand. Make sure you have a prescription from your doctor if you will be carrying syringes, insulin, any narcotic drugs or even codeine, which is illegal in Greece, though nowadays luggage searches for the popular USA compound empirin-codeine are essentially unknown. Interestingly, cannabis supplements containing CBD are legal here (Cannaboss is a major producer; www.cannaboss.gr) and can be bought at certain shops. Non-medical cannabis, though, is another matter.

D

DRIVING

Road conditions. Kefaloniá has a deserved reputation for having some of the most challenging roads in Greece. Surfaces on main roads are generally very good, though curves in the road are often indicated too late (or not at all) and are rarely banked correctly. If there is a mirror on a bend, downshift; it is probably going to be extremely tight or narrow, or perhaps both, with or without oncoming traffic.

On clifftop roads it is too dangerous to overtake, so be patient if there is a slow-moving bus or heavy vehicle in front of you. Conversely, try to let local speed demons pass you as soon as it is safe to do so.

Kefalonian secondary roads are some of the narrowest on any of the Greek islands – it's difficult to safely exceed 50kph (31mph) – while anything marked 'unsurfaced' on a map can be very rough indeed. Rockslides are common during or just after the rainy season, and broken-up verges/shoulders or potholes are not unknown on even the best-paved stretches. Drive with extreme caution, as you might be held responsible for damage sustained to the underside or windshield of your hire car, even with comprehensive coverage.

Driving regulations. Drive on the right and pass on the left. Traffic from the right has right of way. A Greek practice to be aware of is that if a driver flashes the lights. On a narrow road, it usually means 'Stay where you are, I'm coming through', not 'Go ahead'. (Occasionally it may mean 'Beware, traffic police control ahead!') Seat belts are obligatory, as is having your driving licence on

---

Are we on the right road for…? **Páme kalá yia…?**
Fill the tank please, with (low-test, 95 octane) petrol **Parakaló, gemíste tin me enenindapendári**
My car has broken down **To avtokínito mou éhi páthi vlávi**
There's been an accident **Éhei gine éna atýhima**

you while at the wheel; there is a €200 fine if you are caught without it. The speed limit is 50kph (31mph) inside built-up areas (Argostóli and all resorts), 80kph (50mph) in the countryside. In practice, however, rural road conditions set their own speed limit.

Other drivers constitute a major hazard. Greeks love to straddle the median line, barge out recklessly from side-roads, or overtake on either side. One-way street systems are often regarded as optional, especially by two-wheeled drivers.

Breathalyser stops for drink-driving are very common on weekend nights and Sunday afternoon.

Fuel. Generally you will never be far from a filling station near Argostóli and along the main roads in the south and east of Kefaloniá, but in parts of the north and southwest of Kefaloniá, they are few and far between. Keep your tank full, especially if driving to the far northern end of the island, which of necessity involves being in low, fuel-consuming gear much of the time. Note that in rural areas filling stations are open only until about 8pm, and most close on Sunday. On busy main roads and in resorts they open daily from early until late. There is at least one filling station, east of Argostóli that has after-hours automatic-sales pumps, accepting debit/credit cards or euro notes.

If you need help. Your car hire office should provide contact numbers for breakdown service. If you are involved in an accident with another vehicle and/or with significant personal injury or property damage, it is illegal to leave

Detour Παράκαμψη/**Parákampsi**
Parking Παρκιγκ/**Párking**
No parking Απαγορεύεται/**Apagorévete to párking**
Be careful Προσοχή/**Prosohí**
Bus stop Στάση λεοφορείου/**Stási leoforíou**
For pedestrians Για πεζούς/**Yia pezoús**
Danger, dangerous Κίνδυνος, επικίνδυνος/**Kíndynos, epikíndhynos**
Entry forbidden Απαγορεύεται η είσοδος/**Apagorévete i ísodhos**

the scene – wait for the ordinary police or traffic police *(trohéa)* to show up, breathalyse all drivers and take statements.

Road signs. On main roads and at junctions these will be in Greek and Latin letters; on secondary roads they may just be in Greek (for some important ones see the list). Critical junctions can be atrociously indicated, with vital signs sometimes either uprooted or hidden by foliage.

E

ELECTRICITY

Greece has 220-volt/50-cycle AC current out of European Type F (earthed, heavy-duty apparatus) or Type C (unearthed) two-pin sockets, so bring an adapter or transformer with you as necessary (though plug adaptors can be found at better-stocked electrical goods merchants).

> a transformer **énas metashimatistís**
> an adapter **énas prosarmostís**

EMBASSIES AND CONSULATES

Embassies *(presvíes)* or full consulates *(proxenía)* are all located in Athens.

Australian Embassy: Hatziyianni Mexi 5, Level 2, by the Hilton Hotel, 115 28 Athens, tel: 210 870 4000, https://greece.embassy.gov.au

British Embassy: Ploutárhou 1, 106 75 Athens, tel: 210 72 72 600, www.gov. uk/world/organisations/british-embassy-athens

Canadian Embassy: Ethnikís Andistáseos 48, Halándri, 152 31 Athens; tel: 210 72 73 400, www.canadainternational.gc.ca/greece-grece

Irish Embassy Vassiléos Konstandínou 7, 106 74 Athens, tel: 210 72 32 771/2, www.dfa.ie/embassies/irish-embassies-abroad/europe/greece/

South African Embassy and Consulate: Kifisías 60, 151 25 Maroúsi, Athens, tel: 210 6179 020

US Embassy and Consulate: Vassilísis Sofías 91, 101 60 Athens, tel: 210 72 12 951, https://gr.usembassy.gov

EMERGENCIES

Police: (universal emergency number) 100; (Argostóli Town) 26710 22100.
Hospitals: (Argostóli) tel 26713 61100, www.kefalonia-hospital.gr/en.
Ambulance: 166.
Fire Reporting: 199.
Port Authorities: (Argostóli) 26950 28118; Póros 26740 72460; Sámi 26740 22031; Fiskárdho 26740 41400. Be aware that ringing these numbers may result only in a recorded message in Greek concerning that days arrivals and departures. It is generally more productive to visit them in person.

G

GETTING AROUND

The local bus consortium (KTEL, https://ktelkefalonias.gr has a list of local routes and frequencies, which tend be fairly sparse.

GETTING THERE

It is possible to cross Europe overland and take the ferry from Italy to Pátra on the Greek mainland and then from Kyllíni, further down the coast, to either Póros or (less frequently) to Argostóli. Most years, there is a peak season service from the Italian port Bári calling at Sámi. Between Sámi and Pisaetós on Itháki there are typically three daily sailings in each direction.

From the UK, travellers can fly directly into Kefaloniá on easyJet (www.easyjet.com) from a number of airports, including Bristol, from May to Sept or British Airways (ba.com) from London Heathrow between late May and early October – if you choose not to use the charter flight provided by package operators. Out of season, visitors will have to fly to Athens first, from where there are domestic flights on Greek airline Olympic (one or two daily; www.olympicair.com), or Sky Express (www.skyexpress.gr) to Kefaloniá (at least one daily, 65 mins).

H

HEALTH AND MEDICAL CARE

In theory, UK citizens with a Global Health Insurance Card (obtainable free online at https://www.nhs.uk/using-the-nhs/healthcare-abroad/apply-for-a-free-uk-global-health-insurance-card-ghic) can get free treatment under the Greek health service. However, you are likely to receive the minimum treatment; medication must be paid for (although the prescription itself should be free from a state doctor) and state hospital facilities are over-stretched in the tourist season. It's therefore preferable to obtain private medical insurance for your holiday. Doctors and dentists are concentrated in Argostóli; your hotel or apartment owner will be able to find you one who speaks English. Some resorts have a local, private medical clinic – most public ones have closed.

Hospital. The hospital on Kefaloniá is at Souidhías 17 in Argostóli (tel; 26713 61100, www.kefalonia-hospital.gr/en), operating a 24-hour emergency service.

Pharmacies. A green cross on a white background identifies a pharmacy (ΦΑΡΜΑΚΕΙΟ – *farmakío*). They are normally open only 9am–2.30pm Monday to Friday but a notice on the door should tell you the nearest one for after-hours service. One pharmacy is always open in Argostóli at night and on Saturday and Sunday. Without a prescription, you can't get sleeping pills, antibiotics or certain medicines for stomach upsets.

While swimming near rocks look out for sea urchins – their black spines

a doctor/dentist **énas yiatrós/odontíatros**
hospital **nosokomío**
indigestion **varystomahiá**
sunstroke **ilíasi**
a fever **pyretós**

are very sharp and will break off in your skin. If this happens, seek medical attention, as they are very tricky to remove, but need to be; left unattended, the entry point and area below festers, since the hollow spines act as ideal conduits for microbes.

L

LANGUAGE

Only in remote countryside spots will non-Greek-speaking tourists possibly run into serious communication problems. You will find that basic English is spoken almost everywhere, as are Italian, German and French, to some degree.

Stress is a very important feature of the Greek language, denoted by an accent above the vowel of the syllable to be emphasised. We have indicated proper stress in all of our transliterations of multi-syllable words.

The table lists the Greek letters in their upper- and lower-case forms, followed by the closest individual or combined letters to which they correspond in English

Doubled letters		
ΑΙ αι	ey	as in *they*
ΑΥ αυ	av	as in *avant-garde*
ΕΙ ει	i	as in *ski*
ΓΚ γκ	Hard g	*when initial, 'ng' as in longer when medial*
ΟΥ ου	ou	as in *soup*
ΓΓ γγ	ng	*as in longer; always medial*
ΓΞ γξ	nx	*as in anxious; always medial*
ΜΠ μπ	b	*if initial, mb when medial*
ΝΤ ντ	ντ	*d if initial, nd when medial*

A	α	a	as in **fa**ther
B	β	v	as in **v**eto
Γ	γ	y	as in go (except pronounced 'y' before 'e' and 'i' sounds, when it's like the y in **y**es)
Δ	δ	dh	like th in then
E	ε	e	as in get
Z	ζ	z	as in English
H	η	i	as in ski
Θ	θ	th	like th in thin
I	ι	i	as in ski
K	κ	k	as in English
Λ	λ	l	as in English
M	μ	m	as in English
N	ν	n	as in English
Ξ	ξ	x	as in exercise
O	o	o	as in *road*
Π	π	p	as in English
P	ρ	r	as in English but rolled more
Σ	σ/ς	s	as in *ki**ss***, except like z before m or g sounds
T	τ	t	as in English
Y	υ	y	as in country
Φ	φ	f	as in English
X	χ	h	as in Scottish 'loch'
Ψ	ψ	ps	as in tipsy
Ω	ω	o	as in b**o**ne

LGBTQ+ TRAVELLERS

Kefaloniá has no specific gay scene, but attitudes in resorts are generally relaxed. Be discreet in conservative rural communities. Homosexual practice is legal in Greece for people aged 17 and older.

M

MAPS

The best map available of Kefaloniá and Itháki is issued by Anavasi (https://anavasi.gr/maps-gr/cephalonia-ithaki-chartis-gr), at a scale of 1:65,000 for Kefaloniá and 1:25,000 for Itháki. It may be available locally at newsagents or tourist shops. Both the Anavasi map and the Freytag-Berndt 1:50,000 Kefaloniá map are available online from www.themapcentre.com. Free tourist maps of far inferior quality are widely available, for example from car hire offices.

MEDIA

Newspapers and magazines *(efimerídhes; periodhiká)*. During the tourist season, foreign-language newspapers are on sale at shops and kiosks on the island, generally available the same day. Greek news in English can be found at www.ekathimerini.com and https://greekreporter.com/greek news.

Television *(tiliórasi)*. Most hotels and many bars offer satellite television networks, including CNN, BBC World and, in the busier resorts, Sky.

Radio. BBC World Service is no longer broadcast on short wave but can be streamed on www.bbc.co.uk. Note that live sports events will not be broadcast.

MONEY

Currency *(nómisma)*. In common with most other Western European countries, the euro (EUR or €) is the official currency used in Greece. Notes are in denominations of 5, 10, 20, 50, 100 and 200 euros; coins in 1 and 2 euros and 1, 2, 5, 10, 20 and 50 cents, known as *leptá* in Greek. Notes of 100 euros and above are regarded with suspicion, as possibly counterfeit, and can often only be exchanged in banks. 500-euro notes were withdrawn from circulation in 2018 because of their popularity with mega-criminals.

Banks and currency exchange. You'll find banks in Argostóli; the Bank of Greece at Momferátou 17 is the best place to change paper notes, with no or low commission. Exchange rates appear on a digital display, and are identical for all banks. Major hotels and a scant few travel agencies (the latter sometimes called 'tourist offices') are authorised to change money, but you will probably get less for your money than you would from a bank even if the service is advertised as 'commission free'.

ATMs. The easiest method to obtain cash is through 'hole-in-the-wall' cash dispensers. These can be found in Argostóli and in some of the larger resorts. Depending upon your own individual card fees, this might also be the cheapest way to get money.

Credit and debit cards: As part of the Greek government's campaign to stamp out the thriving black economy, card transactions are actively encouraged at hotels, tavernas, supermarkets and filling stations. Surprisingly unlikely-looking enterprises have the necessary device, though American Express and Diners Club enjoy almost no acceptance.

> I want to change some pounds/dollars **Thélo na allákso merikés líres/meriká dollária**
> Do you have a (Point of Sale) card apparatus? **Éhete syskeví POS?** (pronounced 'poss')

O

OPENING TIMES

Mikró ýpno (the Geek early afternoon nap) is still alive and well on Kefaloniá, observed and enforced by law most strictly outside tourist areas. Do not disturb people at home between 3 and 6pm; loud noise (such as music systems, chain saws, revving engines, etc) is prohibited during that time, or before 8am.

Shops. Traditional hours are generally Mon–Sat 8.30 or 9am–2 or 2.30pm. On Tuesday, Thursday and Friday shops reopen in the evening from 5.30 or 6pm until 8.30–9pm. Shops catering to tourists often stay open all through the day and until late each evening, as well as part of Sunday. Larger supermarkets open Mon–Fri 8.30am–9pm and Sat 9am–8pm; in resort areas you will find at least one supermarket with Sunday hours (typically 9am–2pm or 10am–4pm).

Museums and tourist attractions. State-run museums are closed on Tuesday, and typically open Wed–Sat 8.30am–3.30pm and Sun 8.30 or 9.30am–2.30 or 3pm. Private museums are less reliable, typically shut Sat/Sun, and often must be phoned to book a visit.

Banks. Mon–Fri 8am–2pm.

Businesses and offices. 8am–1pm, then 2–5pm. Government offices work 8am–1.30pm, sometimes 2pm, and don't reopen.

Restaurants and tavernas. More traditional establishments open for lunch from noon until around 3.30pm and for dinner from 7pm to 11.15pm or even a bit later.

P

POLICE

Emergency telephone number: **100**.

Argostóli station: Far south edge of town, tel: 26710 22433 or 27836.

Traffic police check car documents and driving licences, operate speed and drunk traps and issue fines for illegal parking (fines in Greece are high). Car-hire companies will use your credit-card details to pay ignored parking tickets; you have 10 working days to pay moving violations in person. Failing that, a court date will be set, and a summons sent to your home address. Failure to appear will result in an extra conviction for contempt of court, and make future re-entry to Greece potentially difficult.

> Where's the nearest police station? **Pou íne to kondinótero astynomikó tmíma?**

POST OFFICES

Post offices (labelled ΕΛΤΑ for Elliniká Tahydhromía) handle letters, parcels and money orders but don't exchange foreign currency. Look for a blue sign with a stylised head of Hermes traced on it in yellow.

Post offices are generally open Mon–Fri 7.30am–2pm. Registered letters and parcels to non-EU destinations are checked before being sent, so don't seal them until presenting them at the desk. The main post office in Argostóli is at Lithóstroto 19 (Mon–Fri 7.30am–4pm), one block inland from the shoreline boulevard.

Letterboxes are yellow but if there are two slots, make sure you use the one marked *exoterikó* (abroad). In tourist hotels, the receptionist will take care of dispatching your mail. It is best to leave letters at a proper post office, since most letterboxes have fairly infrequent collections.

a stamp for this letter/postcard **éna grammatósimo giaftó to grámma/giaftí tin kart postál**
registered, recorded **systiméno**

PUBLIC HOLIDAYS

Banks, offices and shops are closed on the following national holidays, as well as during some feast days and festivals (see also What's On page 73):
1 January *Protohroniá* New Year's Day
6 January *Ágia Theofánia* Epiphany
25 March *Ikostipémpti Martíou (tou Evangelismoú)* Annunciation and Greek Independence Day
1 May *Protomagiá* May Day
15 August *Dhekapendávgoustos* Dormition of the Panagía Day
28 October *Ikostiogdhóïs Oktovríou Óhi* ('No') Day, celebrates defiance of the 1940 Italian ultimatum
25 December *Hristoúgenna* Christmas Day; 26 December is also an official holiday
Moveable dates:

Kathará Dheftéra 1st day of Lent: 'Clean Monday'
Megáli Paraskeví Good Friday
Páskha Easter Sunday
Tou Agíou Pnévmatos Whit (Pentecost) Sunday and Monday ('Holy Spirit'), end May or early/mid-June
Note: These moveable holidays are celebrated according to dates in the Greek Orthodox calendar, which usually differ from Catholic or Protestant dates.

R

RELIGION

The national religion of Greece is Greek Orthodoxy. You must dress modestly to visit churches and monasteries, which normally means long trousers for men, a long skirt or trousers for women and covered shoulders for both sexes. However, men are often allowed to wear long shorts (over the knees) and skirts or wraps may be provided at the entry to churches for women to cover themselves.

In Argostóli, the church of St Nicholas on the Lithóstroto is Catholic, and open year-round for residents and visitors.

S

SMOKING

Since 2010, it has been illegal to smoke in any indoor space in Greece, including tavernas and bars. For a nation of inveterate puffers (though smoking is down in recent decades), compliance with the law is surprisingly well adhered to. But smoking is still allowed on open-air terraces or patios, so such spaces are in high demand, even during cooler weather. When you see ashtrays set out, you can be sure that the owner will not chivvy you for indulging inside, though they risk substantial fines from inspectors if one should come along. Vaping is also big business in Greece, and subject to the same strictures as smoking tobacco.

T

TELEPHONES

Local calling. There are no longer any area codes as such in Greece; even within the same local-call zone you must dial all 10 digits of the land-line number. What were the old codes are now merely locators: 26710 and 26711 for Argostóli and environs, plus the Palikí Peninsula; 26740 for the east coast, Itháki, Ássos and the Fiskárdho region. All Greek mobiles start with '69' and also total ten digits.

From overseas. To call Greece from abroad, first dial the international access code (00 from the UK, 011 from North America), then **30** (the country code for Greece) and finally all 10 digits of the local number, be it land or mobile/cell.

Long distance from Greece. International direct dialling is available at very rare, noisy street-corner phone booths. These take phonecards (*tilekártes*), which are quite good value, as well as credit/debit cards. Pre-paid VoIP calling cards with a freephone access code and scratch-off PIN number are more common; they can be used from any phone and are by far the cheapest way to call abroad. To reverse charges (collect calls), dial 151 for Europe and 161 for the rest of the world. For overseas directory assistance, dial the international operator on 139. For the local operator, dial 132. If your home mobile plan allows free or cheap roaming while in Greece, that is really the simplest, least expensive method of calling abroad while there.

reverse-charge (collect) call **pirotéo apó to paralípti**

TIME ZONES

Greek time is GMT plus two hours. Daylight saving, when Greek clocks are put forward one hour, is observed from 3am on the last Sunday of March to 3am on the last Sunday of October. The chart shows the times in Greece and various other places during the European summer.

Los Angeles	New York	London	Paris	**Greece**	Sydney	Auckland
2am	5am	10am	11am	**noon**	8pm	9pm

TIPPING

Greeks aren't obsessed with tipping, but do leave a little more if service has been good, or the kérazma was particularly sumptuous. Usual amounts are as follows: hotel porter, €1 per bag; hotel room cleaner, €1 per day; waiter, 5–10 percent; taxi driver, just round up the meter amount; hairdresser/barber, 10 percent; lavatory attendant, €0.40–0.50.

TOILETS

Public conveniences are rare and best avoided. A better option is to use facilities at museums or the better cafés. If you do drop in specifically to use the toilet, it's customary to purchase a coffee or some other drink before leaving.

Important note: you are always expected to put toilet tissue in the waste bin rather than down the toilet. Due to their narrow-bore drain-pipes, toilets easily become clogged, and in rural areas it all goes to a soak pit which can't digest paper.

Where is the toilet? **Pou íne i toualétta?**
There's no paper!! **Dhen ehei hárti toualéttas!!**

TOURIST INFORMATION

Kefaloniá does not have an official tourism office, but the national Visit Greece entity (www.visitgreece.gr; still sometimes known as the Greek National Tourist Organisation or EOT in Greek) has the following offices abroad:

UK and Ireland: 5th Floor East, Great Portland House, 4 Great Portland Street, London W1W 8QJ; tel: (020) 7495 9300.

US and Canada: 800 Third Avenue, 23rd Floor, New York, NY 10022; tel: (212) 421 5777.

These offices supply general information and glossy pictures, but when it comes to anything specific on Kefaloniá they are usually of little help.

TRANSPORT

Buses (*leoforía*). The public bus service on Kefaloniá is patchy but, where it does exist, is very good value; routes and frequencies are sharply reduced outside of tourist season. Timetables are displayed at the KTEL bus station in Argostóli (tel: 26710 22281, https://ktelkefalonias.gr), located at Andóni Trítsi 5, the far southeast end of the waterfront. For all buses, buy your tickets from Argostóli station or on board out in the countryside. You can flag a bus down or disembark anywhere within reason, though ideally at a signed stop (ΣΤΑΣΕΙΣ – *stásis*).

Taxis. These are an expensive way to get around but may be your only option in parts of Kefaloniá. Make sure the meter is switched on; there are two rates depending on time of day and whether you are in or out of town. Large baggage in the boot attracts a surcharge of about €0.40 per item. Radio taxis can be summoned, for which there's also a small surcharge. Kefalonia Taxi (tel: 26711 05178; https://kefaloniataxi.gr) and Kefalonia Airport Taxi (tel: 6986 742385; https://kefaloniataxis.com) are two major services with online booking capability.

Ferries. Frequent ferries run between Kyllíni on the mainland and Póros on the southeast coast, less frequently bertween Kyllíni and Argostóli. There is also a regular seasonal ferry (two daily May–Sept) between Pessádha on the south coast and Ágios Nikólaos (Skinári), in the north of Zákynthos. There are regular ferries between Sámi and Itháki, and also between those two points and Astakós on the central mainland. For current local ferry schedules and fares consult https://zasferries.com/kefalonia; the port authority (see page 105) or online at www.gtp.gr, though this last is far from infallible.

> What's the fare to…? **Póso éhi éna isitírio giá…?**
> When's the next bus to…? **Póte févgi to epómeno leoforío yiá…?**

V

VISAS AND ENTRY REQUIREMENTS

All EU citizens may enter Greece to visit or work for an unlimited length of time. Citizens of Ireland can enter with a valid identity card or passport. British citizens must be in possession of a valid full passport, which will be stamped upon entry and exit. As post-Brexit tourists, Brits are subject to Schengen Zone rules for length of stay – 90 days cumulative in any 180-day period. Fines for overstaying are horrendous, and any excuse short of documented confinement in hospital will not be entertained by officialdom.

Citizens of the US, Canada, Australia and New Zealand can stay for up to three months on production of a valid passport, with no advance visa required. South African citizens require a Schengen Visa, obtained in advance from a Greek embassy or full consulate. If you wish to extend these time-scales you must obtain a permit from the proper department of the Argostóli police station.

Greece has strict regulations about importing drugs. All the obvious ones are illegal, and there are serious consequences for rule-breakers. Codeine and some tranquillisers are also banned, though the days of luggage searches for the popular USA compound empirin-codeine appear to be over. If you take any drug on the advice of your doctor, carry enough for your trip in the official pharmacy container, as medicines for personal use are permitted.

Since the abolition of duty-free allowances for all EU countries, all goods brought into Greece must be duty-paid unless they are for personal use, not resale. In theory there are no limitations to the amount of duty-paid goods that can be brought into the country. However, cigarettes and most spirits are much cheaper in Greece than in Britain and Ireland (government duty is much lower, so waiting until you reach your destination to buy these goods will save you money).

For citizens of non-EU countries, including the UK, allowances for duty-free goods brought into Greece are: 200 cigarettes or 50 cigars or 250g of tobacco; 1 litre of spirits or 4 litres of wine; 250ml of cologne or 50ml of perfume.

Non-EU residents can claim back Value Added Tax (currently between 6 and 24 percent, in Greek ΦΠΑ) on any items costing over €120, provided they export the item within 90 days of purchase. Tax-rebate forms are available only at certain tourist shops and in-town merchants. Keep the receipt and the form, and make your claim at the customs area of your departure airport.

Currency restrictions. There are no limits on the amount of euros visitors can import or export. Cash sums of more than $10,000/€10,000 or equivalent should be declared upon entry.

COVID-19 protocols. As present, Greece has suspended its prior requirement for inbound travellers to present evidence of having had at least three recognised Covid inoculations, or a negative rapid antigen test result no older than two days before arrival date/negative PCR test result no older than three days before arrival. However, should there be a major resurgence of the disease in 2023–24, expect these or similar rules to be re-introduced, so it would be prudent to still travel with such documentation. Additionally, arrivals may again need to fill out an online Greek government Passenger Locator Form a day or two before travel, at https://travel.gov.gr.

W

WEBSITES AND INTERNET ACCESS

Wi-Fi and internet cafés. Since Wi-Fi is now available at just about all accommodation (sometimes charged for at fancier hotels) and almost all cafés/bars/restaurants, very few internet cafés remain. You are much better off with your phone or a tablet device within a wi-fi zone.

What's the code for your wi-fi? **Piós íne o kodikós gia to wi-fi?**

There are various useful websites for people travelling to Kefaloniá or Itháki:
www.visitgreece.gr/islands/ionian-islands/kefalonia The Kefaloniá page of the official Greek tourism entity.
https://www.discovergreece.com/travel-ideas/cover-story/foodie-guide-kefalonia This gastronomic guide tells you what to eat and drink, and where to find it on the island.
https://greecetravelideas.com/guide-to-ithaca-greece-the-island-of-odysseus Greece Travel Ideas has a good page on Itháki.
https://www.greeka.com/ionian/kefalonia/about Long-running site for all things Greek.
www.ithacagreece.com Full of commercial links, but good destination information, especially for beaches.
www.kefalonia-island.com Good roundup of the beaches, and certain villages, plus of course links to accommodation.
http://kefalonia-island.gr/info.php Good descriptions of Kefaloniá attractions.
Matt Barrett, who has been doing online guides to Greece since the mid-1990s, has dedicated pages for both Kefaloniá and Itháki: https://www.greektravel.com/greekislands/kefalonia/index.htm https://www.greektravel.com/greekislands/ithaki/index.htm
https://visitkefalonia.eu Heavily linked to local businesses but good destination information.

WHERE TO STAY

Hotels are rated from 2-star to 5-star, an assessment based more on their common areas and amenities than the actual rooms. Prices can vary widely within each category, while ultra-luxury (5-star) establishments are not price controlled. Thus, a 3-star hotel room may be just as comfortable as a 5-star room, but common areas will not include a conference room, hairdresser, gym, spa or multiple restaurants. All hotels of 3-star rating and above are reasonably furnished, have en-suite rooms and should provide breakfast; rates given, unless specified otherwise, are quoted on a B&B basis. Breakfast is typically buffet-style, with a mix of fruit pieces, juice, cereals, bread and/or cake, cold and warm dishes, plus often a 'live cooking' point where you can order pancakes, waffles or an omelette.

In high summer some form of air conditioning should enable you to get a good night's sleep. If your room doesn't have air conditioning (and a bare handful of the oldest properties still don't), there will either be a ceiling fan or you might be able to obtain a floor-standing fan from reception or the owner. Some rooms may also have mosquito nets on the windows so you can open them in cooler hours without the risk of letting them in.

The majority of the hotels listed following can be found on generic third-party booking sites, but many have their own websites which offer substantial discounts for direct booking. Although finding a room at short notice or on spec is not a problem for much of the year, it is still wise to reserve well in advance for the peak season of late June through early September. To telephone a hotel, dial the international country code for Greece (30), followed by the 10-digit number provided in our listings.

Ratings are based on minimum price rates but prices can often vary widely within each class according to the season, location and availability of rooms. By law, current rates must always be posted in all rooms, usually on the main door or inside the closet; in practice this requirement is often ignored.

The price categories below are for a double room or studio per night in high season, excluding August super peak periods. All hotel unit rates include VAT (Value Added Tax) of 13 percent. Most hotels in beach resorts are only open from April or May through October, and often not as long as that – think June to September. Those in Argostóli are open all year round.

€€€€	above 300 euros
€€€	151–300 euros
€€	80–150 euros
€	below 80 euros

Argostóli and Lássi

Aenos Hotel €€€ *Platía Vallianoú, Argostóli,* https://aenoshotel.com/en. Uncluttered pastel-hued rooms (three categories, also three types of suites) with marble-clad bathrooms sporting butler sinks. The period or reproduction-antique furnishings in the common areas reflect that this was originally an 1847 conversion of the late-18th-century Metaxas family mansion (though all has been rebuilt since 1953). A la carte breakfast included, served out on the plaza, weather permitting.

Ionian Plaza €€ *Platía Valliánou,* https://ionianplaza.com/en. Designer decor throughout, from the lobby up to the cutting-edge bathroom fixtures. Doubles, suites and family units are all on offer. The doubles are a bit on the small side but are adequate given the amount of time you're likely to spend there, and at least one has an outdoor hot-tub. Some balconies overlook the palm-tree-studded plaza. Open all year round but there is a three-night minimum stay in summer. Breakfast included.

Kefalonia Grand €€ for rooms, €€€ for suites *Andóni Trítsi 82, Argostóli,* https://kefaloniagrand.gr. This long-standing seafront property has been totally reinvented as a surprisingly good value boutique hotel, with snazzily designed and comfortable doubles (four grades) and two suites. The on-site restaurant serves tables both outdoors and inside.

Méditerranée €€ rooms, €€€ suites *Lássi,* https://mediterraneehotel.gr. A vast (227 units) 4-star hotel set behind a small strip of beach, 2km (1.2 miles) out of town. Facilities are good and include sizable separate pools for adults and kids, a tennis court, main restaurant plus beach-bar/restaurant and shops. Two categories/price options on offer for both rooms and suites. Open May–early Oct.

Oskars Studios & Apartments €€ *Fanári district, Lássi, Argostóli,* www.oskars.gr. A complex of 15 clean simply furnished studios and apartments for up to five occupants. On-site restaurant and bar. Open all year.

Lixoúri and the south

9 Muses €€€ *Skála, tel: 26710 83563,* https://9museshotel.com. This is an attractively designed bungalow complex of rooms and suites set in well-tended gardens (two pools) just above mid-beach (with amenities there), with the room interiors doing justice to the surroundings. Luxury suites can accommodate up to four, and have jacuzzis.

Captain's House Hotel €€ *Skala,* www.captainshouse.net. Friendly place with just 28 rooms (the ones in the basement are best avoided), a couple of blocks from the resort's main street and not far from the beach. Gym and tennis court on site. Minimum stays three–seven nights depending on season. Open May–mid-Oct

La Cité €€ *Lixoúri,* www.lacitehotellixouri.gr. Four blocks uphill from the harbour, this cheerfully decorated hotel has tastefully and colourfully furnished rooms, a lift to reach the top floor and an odd-shaped swimming pool in its lush, exotic gardens. Bar, but no food service apart from breakfast. Open Apr–Oct.

Melissani € *Sámi, tel: 26740 22464,* www.melissanihotel.gr. Just uphill from the harbour, this friendly place is a tad old-fashioned but offers some of the most reasonably priced rooms on the island. Roof bar offers water views. Open May–Sept.

Odysseus Palace €€ *Póros,* http://kefalonia-hotel.gr/en. This attractive modern hotel is the most comfortable place to stay here. Good discounts may be available for the large and airy units (studios and apartments, including family size ones). Being away from the seafront, this hotel is quieter than most here. Open all year.

Panas Hotel €€ *below Spartiá village,* https://panas-kefalonia.com. A large but pleasant south-coast hotel, close to good Klimatsía beach. The rooms, all of which have a balcony, are fine, if a little unimaginative. The hotel does, however, have good facilities for children, including their own pool and play area. There is also an on-site restaurant and a poolside bar. Open May–Oct.

Santa Irena € *Póros,* http://santa-irena-poros.ionianislandshotels.com/en. Cosy hotel offering compact but bright and comfortable rooms at unbeatable prices; a good choice before an early-morning ferry out. Quiet inland location, a few blocks from the seafront. Open July–early Sept only.

Hotel Summery €€ *Grigoríou Lambráki 36, Lixoúri,* https://summery.gr. Large but quiet 3-star hotel on Lixoúri's small beach, south of the town centre. Rooms are showing their age, though many have balconies. Fair-sized pool with day-beds around it, which may appeal more than the scrappy beach. Town-view units are cheaper.

Tara Beach €€ *Skála,* http://tarabeach.gr. A large but unobtrusive hotel set in lush gardens behind an excellent beach. The soothingly coloured rooms sport contemporary design touches, and if you can't be bothered to waddle the few metres to the sea with its sunbeds, there is a good pool-with-bar in the pleasant gardens. On-site snack bar, but no full-service restaurant.

Trapezáki Bay Hotel €€ *500 metres above Trapezáki beach,* https://trapezakibayhotel.com. Upmarket, adults-only resort with a full range of amenities, including medium-sized pool, restaurant, bar and a spa with all imaginable treatments and subtly appointed rooms. Their policy of maintaining one price all season, airport transfer and breakfast included, makes it especially good value in high summer. Open May–Oct.

The north

Agnantia B&B €€, but €€€ for premium suite *Tselendáta hamlet, 3km (2 miles) from Fiskárdho on the minor road towards Mánganos,* tel: 26740 51801, www.agnantia.com. Very well maintained and improbably located, these hillside rooms and suites make for a lovely stay. As well as friendly, efficient service, tasteful, comfortable units offer kitchenettes, and most have balconies with knockout views over to Itháki. A good, and generous, breakfast, featuring proprietress Myra's pies, cakes and *marmelades* is included.

Archontiko €€€ *Fiskárdho, south quay, tel: 26740 41342,* https://archontiko-fiskardo.gr/el. Splendidly converted stone mansion backing onto the harbour. The furniture in luxurious rooms is period style, but all other appointments are cutting edge. There are a couple of rooms overlooking the harbour but noise comes with the view. Open Apr–Oct.

Athina Beach €€ *Karavómylos, tel: 26740 22779,* https://athinahotel.gr. Barely 2km (1.2 miles) west of Sámi, close to a fine beach, this well-maintained 3-star hotel is easily the best place to stay on the bay. There is a fair-sized pool on site; rooms, studios and an apartment are spacious; and the service is good.

Emelisse Nature Resort €€€€ *Émblysi beach, 10-minute walk north of Fiskárdho, tel: 26740 41200,* www.emelisseresort.com. This child-friendly, upmarket boutique hotel offfers luxurious, Asian-flavoured rooms, suites, apartments of varying sizes and maisonettes. Inevitably, the infinity pool terrace has a lovely view. On-site gym and Elemis-branded spa. For this price you should expect to be pampered, and service lives up to expectations. Three-night minimum stay.

Kanakis Apartments €€ *Ássos,* https://kanakisapartments.gr. Very smart, well-designed self-catering suites, one-bedroom apartments and larger maisonettes, all tastefully appointed in cool pastel hues, sharing a pool and sweeping views. Only a 100m walk into the heart of the village. Open April–Oct, with a minimum three-night stay. Breakfast (in your unit) is charged extra.

Mina's Apartments € *Dhivaráta, tel: 26740 61515,* www.minasapartments.gr. Just above the main junction in Dhivaráta, these spacious and well-furnished studios (12) and apartments (two) are easily the best of the limited accommodation options close to Mýrtos beach, and also well placed for car-touring the entire island.

Odyssey €€€ *Agía Evfimía, tel: 26740 61060,* http://hotelodyssey.gr. This adults-only boutique hotel lies round the headland from the harbour, offering spacious sea-view suites plus a restaurant, bar, spa, gym and huge pool. Two-night minimum stay. May–Sept.

Regina's € *Fiskárdo, tel: 26740 41125,* www.regina-studios.gr. Simple but comfortable studios (plus one family apartment accommodating seven guests at a pinch) at the southern edge of the village, near the car park. There's a well-kept garden courtyard; the family that runs the place is very hospitable. Some units have balconies looking over the village to the bay; the best deal in this upmarket resort, Co-managed with the local small-boat rental oufit. Open April–Oct.

Vathý, Itháki

Captain Yiannis €€ https://captainyiannis.com. Complete with tennis court and pool with bar, this great-value resort round the east side of the bay is spread over several blocks of modern rooms and suites, done up in earthy and pastel tones. Breakfast included. Open mid-May to Sept.

Mentor € http://hotelmentor.gr. The town's oldest (built 1969) hotel, in the southeast corner of the harbour, was last refurbished in 2011. Its comfortable, cheerfully decorated rooms (including four suites) have balconies either with direct or side views of the water. Breakfast included.

Omirikon Residence €€ *On the east side of the bay, between the Mentor hotel and Captain Yiannis resort,* http://hotelomirikon.com. Stylish boutique hotel that maintains a personal, family-run touch. All units here are categorized as suites that are pleasingly spacious and well furnished with lovely sea-view balconies and perfectly functional kitchenettes. Breakfast is included. Open May–Oct.

Kióni, Itháki

Captain's Apartments € *Kióni,* http://captains-apartments.gr. Set well above the village, with sweeping views of the bay, these spacious studios and apartments cater for up to three people and are decorated in warm rustic colours. Open May–Sept.

INDEX

THE **MINI** ROUGH GUIDE TO
KEFALONIÁ

First edition 2023

Editors: Kate Drynan, Rachel Lawrence
Author: Marc Dubin
Picture Editor: Tom Smyth
Cartography Update: Carte
Layout: Pradeep Thapliyal
Head of DTP and Pre-Press: Katie Bennett
Head of Publishing: Kate Drynan
Photography Credits: Alamy 31; Bigstock
7B; Britta Jaschinski/Apa Publications 71, 82;
Cephalonia Botanica 36; ChristosV 4TL; Fotolia
77; iStock 4TC, 4MC, 4MC, 4TL, 5M, 16, 28, 35,
42, 45, 56, 57, 58, 60, 78; Kevin Cummins/Apa
Publications 12, 14, 23, 31, 33, 41, 46, 48, 51,
53, 55, 66, 72, 81; Mockford & Bonnetti/Apa
Publications 38; Praxinoa 4BL; Shutterstock 1;
4ML, 5M, 5T, 6T, 6B, 7T, 13, 18, 22, 37, 39, 61,
62, 64, 68
Cover Credits: Assos **Igor Tichonow/
Shutterstock**

Distribution
UK, Ireland and Europe: Apa Publications (UK)
Ltd; sales@roughguides.com
United States and Canada: Ingram Publisher
Services; ips@ingramcontent.com
Australia and New Zealand: Booktopia;
retailer@booktopia.com.au
Worldwide: Apa Publications (UK) Ltd; sales@
roughguides.com

**Special Sales, Content Licensing
and CoPublishing**
Rough Guides can be purchased in bulk
quantities at discounted prices. We can create
special editions, personalised jackets and
corporate imprints tailored to your needs. sales@
roughguides.com; http://roughguides.com

This book was produced using **Typefi** automated
publishing software.

Printed in Czech Republic

Contact us
Every effort has been made to provide accurate
information in this publication, but changes
are inevitable. The publisher cannot be held
responsible for any resulting loss, inconvenience
or injury sustained by any traveller as a result
of information or advice contained in the
guide. We would appreciate it if readers would
call our attention to any errors or outdated
information, or if you feel we've left something
out. Please send your comments with the subject
line "Rough Guide Mini Kefaloniá Update" to
mail@uk.roughguides.com.